CW01082210

THE RO. ... .RY OF LOVE

Classical World Series

The Roman Poetry of Love

Elegy and Politics in a
Time of Revolution

Efrossini Spentzou

B L O O M S B U R Y
LONDON • NEW DELHI • NEW YORK • SYDNEY

Bloomsbury Academic

An imprint of Bloomsbury Publishing Plc

50 Bedford Square	1385 Broadway
London	New York
WC1B 3DP	NY 10018
UK	USA

www.bloomsbury.com

Bloomsbury is a registered trade mark of Bloomsbury Publishing Plc

First published 2013

© Efrossini Spentzou, 2013

British Library Cataloguing-in-Publication Data
A catalogue record for this book is available from the British Library.

ISBN: PB: 978-1-78093-204-0
ePub: 978-1-4725-0215-5
ePDF: 978-1-4725-0216-2

Library of Congress Cataloging-in-Publication Data
Spentzou, Efrossini.
The Roman poetry of love : elegy and politics in a time of revolution / Efi Spentzou.
pages cm. -- (Classical world series)
Includes bibliographical references and index.
ISBN 978-1-78093-204-0 (pbk.) -- ISBN 978-1-4725-0215-5
(epub)-- ISBN 978-1-4725-0216-2 (epdf) 1. Love poetry, Latin--History and criticism. 2. Elegiac poetry, Latin--History and criticism.
3. Rome--History--Augustus, 30 B.C.-14 A.D. I. Title.
PA6059.E6S64 2013
874'.01093543--dc23
2013025986

Typeset by Fakenham Prepress Solutions, Fakenham, Norfolk NR21 8NN
Printed and bound in Great Britain

To Richard,

with a thousand kisses and then a hundred
then another thousand and then a second hundred ...

Contents

Preface

Latin love elegy was a genre whose brief poetic candle brightly illuminated the Roman literary world as the Republic was overthrown by a combination of Caesar and Augustus but whose light was seen no more after little more than a generation. Cornelius Gallus is said to have published his now lost elegies c. 50 BCE and the last Ovidian samples of elegiac love poetry were published (after some thorough editing) before the turn of the century. For all its short life, Roman elegy produced spectacular, multifaceted, often difficult poetry. In this short book, I do not provide anything approaching a comprehensive study of the complexities of the genre, but focus on a particular aspect of these poems of love. I highlight (with an eye to those inexperienced in Latin love poetry) the intense affectation of love in these poems. I explore these poems not simply as an expression of a troubled male psychology, which in many ways it is, but also as a reaction to, and a register of, the overwhelming change that swept through Rome and Italy in the transition from the Late Republic to the Augustan Age.

Generic divisions in the study of poetry are often crude and unsatisfactory. Yet, it is the basic proposition of elegy that separates the love poems from other poems of the Augustan period (those of Horace and Virgil, for instance): Roman elegy is marked by a personal voice that dominates the poetry. That voice offers us a portrait of the artist in a confessional mode, an individual transformed (or pretending to be transformed) by powerful emotions. Those emotions distance the man from his surroundings and society, destabilise his social position, and force him in his obsessions to rethink and remake his world under the metamorphosing influence of the *puella*: the girl around whom his life and his poetry orbits in a passionate commitment. Though other plot lines are possible, as we will see when exploring each one of the Latin elegiac poets, the typical Latin love elegy is poetry written to, and for, a specific woman, the poet's mistress, often another man's wife, with whom the poet is hopelessly in love, a love that is often unrequited. In love, the poet makes a new world, but a world not remote or imaginary (not a universe of pastoral idyll), rather a world which is recognisably that of contemporary Rome.

The vehemence of the elegists demands that we downplay the rules of genre and observe the formulae of love, but look through these familiar forms to listen keenly to the voices of the poets. This is not a suggestion to turn back the scholarly clock fifty or so years to a naïve study that would endeavour, in vain, to find the 'real' people, places and events from the narrative of the poems, as if the purpose of reading (and writing) poetry is to discover (and present) historical truths. Over the last decades, considerable effort has gone into exploring the generic conventions and formulations (*topoi*) that hold together the genre, and there are suggestions for further reading on this at the end of the book that reflects this important work. But, if this poetry is not a biography of events, it is also and assuredly not simply a formalist play of conventions and tropes. In this short book, I want to concentrate on the voice of the poet-in-love, this unparalleled thinking-and-speaking in first person that these poems allow, and make some conjectures as to what could be the prompt for this virtuoso, irresistible exercise in self-imaging, however codified, playful or calculated. The voice is real and true in a poetic sense that is not biographical or historical, any more than the poetry of sonnets of Shakespeare or the lyrics of a love song need us to identify the sublime object of affection, the spaces and places of the relationship, or a historic materiality to appreciate their portrayals. The intensity of emotion of all hues (exhilaration, angst, anger, sadness) speaks (to me) of an individual making his way in a new world, whatever the reality of the affairs of the heart that are narrated.

Yet, for all the solipsism of the conventions of the passionate lovers, the poetry is embedded in a very particular political context and is written within a political dynamic that interacts obviously (if with great complexity) with the love narratives of the poetry. Such engagement with the political is a distinctive feature of the elegists' work. Though

Gallus is considered formally the first of the elegists, the earliest
manifestations of the genre, in its special Roman attire, that we have
today are to be found in Catullus' decidedly elegiac sensibility and his
defiant love for a mistress – and Roman matron – Lesbia. A cluster
of those poems about Lesbia is also written in the genre's character-
istic metre, the elegiac couplet. Writing in the late 60s and early 50s,
Catullus' poetry was haunted by the social and political dislocation that
marked the last generation of the Republic. Catullus' world seemed to
be one in flux, in which the old rules either did not apply or could be
ignored. It was a world of wealth, in which Rome's status as the centre
of a world empire was transformative of the values of a conservative,
rural society. Traditional configurations of authority were under threat
and although the new world offered opportunities, those opportunities
were different from those of an earlier age and the shifting structures
of society and the power relations within society had the potential
both to alienate and confuse. The young men of the establishment had
to negotiate this emerging social order, but a new order haunted by
powerful memories of an authoritarian past.

The spectre of Rome's past haunted the Late Republic and virtually
every author of the period invested the past with a moral authority of
a golden age, normally in full recognition of the great distance which
separated the contemporary world from the moral certainties of that
past. For the elite, the conditions of their participation in the political
world (both the right and duty of the Italian aristocracy) were altered
radically, and often inexplicably, in the violent world of the Late
Republic. By the time of Tibullus, the first of our elegiac poets proper,
in the 30s BCE, the shock of the new that we find in Catullus has given
way to a degree of resigned acceptance that the world no longer made
quite the sense it had previously. Propertius' heartaches of the 20s BCE
were played against a backdrop of a world already permeated by a
new imperial sensibility, the implications of which were still unclear,
but would obviously be far reaching. By the time of Ovid, Augustus'
authority had clouded any other possible alternative. All eyes turned
to the emperor and the emperors' eyes ran to the bedrooms and love

affairs of his people. The freedoms of the Late Republic, which Catullus reacted to, were replaced by the disciplines of the Augustan empire.

The transformation from Republic to monarchy in the course of the second half of the first century BCE was the culmination of gradual processes of political, cultural and economic change that manifested itself in periods of intense violence. Octavian/Augustus emerged as victor from the last of the civil wars and was able to establish a stable hegemony in Rome. Nevertheless, Augustus clothed his regime in conservative garb and the social (and political) bases of his power are often obscure. The very nature of the regime has provoked considerable debate among historians. Ronald Syme's provocative book of 1939 described, in somewhat ironic tones, the event as a Roman revolution, but in a very different fashion to the way in which the notion of revolution was deployed in relation to class struggle and the revolutions of the modern era. More recently, Andrew Wallace Hadrill has also deployed the language of revolution, but, perhaps escaping from the shadow of Marxist ownership of the term, has argued that the revolution was cultural: it represented a fundamental alteration of daily life, morality, and an overwhelming shift of authority from sources of knowledge independent of the leader to sources directly subsumed by him. For Wallace Hadrill, the Roman revolution resulted not from political acts or economic transformation (or at least not directly) but from the cultural transformation of Rome in a complex and prolonged engagement with Greek culture.

However we understand the Republican crisis and the subsequent birth of the imperial regime, the transformation was protracted and the mutations that it triggered were general. This was not just a political event, but affected many areas of culture and society. Our elegists were caught in a process of change in which the relationships of the individual and society were thrown into question. Romans were first and foremost citizens, defining themselves, initially at least, in relation to the political community. But when the political community was in itself undergoing radical change, and a change which was seemingly far beyond the influence of any ordinary Roman citizens or even any ordinary member of the Roman aristocracy, the sense of the individual being the plaything of history was overwhelming and destabilising. Times were terrifying and fascinating. The self-remodelling that we find in the elegists reflects a need to self-model because the social and personal relationships of a traditional society were uncertain. In this ever changing, and at times subtly changing, society, everyone was trying new roles. This was a revolution in the sense that the old certainties (and with these, the secure privileges of the Republican ruling class) were no longer available. A transformation of the explicit structures of ruling may even have led to more people gaining access to power, but the status of those involved was increasingly precarious and uncertain as Augustus' personal authority across all areas of life was widening.

This book follows the voice of a cluster of brittle and unsettled wealthy Roman men as they try to exercise their authority and negotiate power within an ever evolving political and social world. But in spite of the political and contextual readings of this poetry which we are encouraged to make, there is an obvious 'excess' in the first-person narrative of these poems that resists categorisation. We cannot resort to binary schemes, such as a private, elegiac voice in open conflict with the public, imperial *dicta*. From the turbulent tail-end years of the Republic that Catullus experienced to the self-confident imperial world that Ovid lived in, these negotiations of power and personal identity evolved often beyond recognition. And yet, the eagerness (and excess) of the poet-lover's own voice remained as a testimony of the poetics of Latin love elegy, exploring and inventing itself in an ever changing world. In that excess, there is an exploration that goes beyond the immediate social context to something that is live and real: the poets find ways of talking through love of the human condition. Love is one of the most powerful and transformative of emotions and in the very timelessness of love, the relationship between the poet and his time is transcended.

In order to stay alert to the intensity of the lover's testimony, I concentrate on the first-person elegiac narratives of love. I leave out altogether Propertius' Book Four (a fascinating book of masks) and Ovid's brilliant generic mutations (the didactic *Art of Love*, and his exile poetry). I have, however, put an Appendix on the single surviving, and now much admired, Roman female elegiac poet, Sulpicia. This is perhaps not enough of an accolade, but I hope that by inserting a parenthesis with her rather jarring voice, I avert the chronic monopolisation of voice and feeling and reaction by upper-class Roman males, however illuminated and reconstructed – or not – they may be. Our elegists tell us one side of the love affair and we, as moderns, cannot ethically read those stories without searching for the female voice.

The aim of this book is to promote thinking and encourage further reading. To this end, I want to highlight some of the least certain aspects of this teasing poetry and try to steer the reader's attention to some of the most intriguing poems – often at the expense of other equally fascinating ones. All translations are my own. I address primarily, but not exclusively, those for whom love elegy is a new discovery, and in so doing, I explore why, I think, we should read poetry two millennia old and why it continues to speak, powerfully, to a world not so different as people might imagine.

Efi Spentzou
April 2013

Catullus: Political Turbulence and Literary Innovation: A Genre is Born in Rome

Let us live my Lesbia, and let us love,
and let us value the talk of old stern men at just one penny.
Suns can set and rise again:
for us, when the day's brief light has set once,
there is one perpetual night waiting to be slept.
Give me a thousand kisses, and then a hundred,
then another thousand, and then a second hundred,
then right after that another thousand, then another hundred,
and when we will have made many thousands,
we will mix them up so that we do not know,
and lest any obnoxious man casts an evil eye on us,
having found out the total amount of the kisses we shared.

Catullus, poem 5, a mere 13 lines, is a heady outburst, a firework of a poem. Passion, thrill, irreverence, aggressiveness, exaggeration and provocation jostle in its brief space. It is an intense and unusual poem. But is it a good poem – in our eyes? in the eyes of the Romans? Why does Catullus invite us to (mis)count his kisses, and if the kisses are counted, who counts and why? Why, and for whom, is there anger in the poet's voice? Who are the grumpy old men? What do they have against the youth, and especially Catullus and his beloved? Was such sexual passion a bad thing for early first-century BCE Rome and its poetry? How do the two themes of the poem, kisses and curses, interrelate? As Catullus sets Roman love poetry on its course, so he sets up the questions that the genre raises. These are the questions that will accompany us throughout this short book: welcome to the world of Latin love elegy.

The end of an era

Our information about Catullus' life is sparse. He was born in Verona in northern Italy c. 84 BCE and died c. 54 BCE. He was the offspring of a wealthy Italian family with connections to the aristocratic circles in Rome, not least to Julius Caesar himself. He was an equestrian, of the second status band in the Roman society, and would have a certain income, probably most of it derived from the estates of his family, which would have brought him a comfortable leisure in which he could practise poetry without worrying too much about making ends meet – and we will come back to this soon. Yet, his relative wealth and his connections meant that he was on the fringe of political circles and that brought with it certain practical worries. Catullus lived in times of major political and social upheaval that marked his life and character (or at least poetic voice) irrevocably. His generation was witnessing (though perhaps they were not fully aware of it) the long, protracted and painful end of an illustrious era: the Republic. In the course of this prolonged demise, society and its values changed beyond recognition and personal life and expectations could not but follow suit. Let us explore a little more what actually happened.

For many, the root of the turmoil that culminated a decade after Catullus' own death with the assassination of Julius Caesar in 44 BCE must be traced back well into the second century BCE. As the Roman Republic grew increasingly dominant in Europe and the Mediterranean, the bedrock of Roman society, the values (and the livelihoods) of the honourable and traditional farmer-soldiers that sustained the Republic for centuries, came to be seen as a thing of the past in an increasingly metropolitan, urbane and wealthy imperial city. Rome's military success brought considerable wealth to the city, but that wealth was not distributed evenly across Roman society. Rome itself grew from being a city state in the centre of Italy to being a world political power with its citizens and subjects located across its vast empire. Rome may have triumphed, but dissatisfaction and alienation were bubbling under the surface.

For much of the last century of the Republic, Rome shifted from one crisis to the next. After every 'solution' there was a brief period in which the problems seemed under control, but then issues would resurface, perhaps manifesting themselves in subtly different ways, but frequently resulting in violence and death. As early as 133 BCE, the social grievances and divisions at the heart of Roman society resulted in an extended period of violence. Tiberius Gracchus, a tribune of the people, attempted to tackle what he and his supporters saw as a long-standing problem: the impoverishment of rural Italy and a subsequent issue with recruitment to the army. Tiberius sought to resolve the poverty of the urban and rural poor through the distribution of public land (a time-honoured procedure), but, as much of the public land was occupied, the measure was controversial. Some saw in Tiberius an ambitious politician seeking to build for himself a powerful base for support among the lower classes of Rome and suspected him of wishing to overthrow the political order and secure for himself a permanent political authority. In an outbreak of political violence, Tiberius and many of his supporters were killed. A decade later, his younger brother Gaius attempted to revive the Gracchan legacy, and enjoyed some considerable success, but he too was to fall victim to conservative elements within the Roman political elite, fearful of his power and contemptuous of his political methods.

Further tribunes followed, attempting to revive the Gracchan policies and challenge the power of the Roman political elite. In the first decades of the first century BCE, the traumatic violence of Roman politics had escalated into civil war. First, Rome and her long-time allies in Italy quarrelled over the political rights of those allies. War resulted, sweeping across much of Italy. Then, the general Sulla found himself at odds with the popular assembly and staged a coup, marching his troops into the city and attempting to find and kill his enemies. One of those enemies was the eminent general Marius, who was forced to flee into exile in Africa. Once Sulla had himself headed east to lead one of Rome's imperial wars, Marius returned, defeated Sulla's men and established his own blood-stained regime. The regime awaited

Sulla's return and the further round of warfare that would result. Sulla's second spell in power did not end the wars. Civil violence spread to Spain and Africa. Disaffected politicians in Rome were brutally eliminated.

Catullus himself would have been too young to have experienced any of these wars, but his parents and elders would have been marked by the traumatic memories and be able to recall the purges of Roman aristocrats and the battles that left so many of all social classes dead across the battlefields of Italy and the empire. Catullus himself would have grown up in the era of the Spartacan revolt. He was a youth when the prominent politician Cicero executed without trial the Catilinarian conspirators and Roman armies clashed in northern Italy. He would have seen the street violence in Rome, led by Clodius, whose sister, Clodia, many think of as the real woman hidden behind Catullus' *puella*, the Lesbia of a thousand kisses. Catullus died shortly before Clodius was murdered in 53 BCE. After Clodius' death, Caesar, returning from Gaul, launched a further civil war against Pompey and his senatorial supporters, and Octavian and his allies nailed down the coffin of the Republic in the wars that followed Caesar's assassination in March 44 BCE.

Rome's military success over the period from c. 300 to c. 49 BCE brought Rome an empire of a size and power never before seen in the Mediterranean world, but in its imperial wealth and prosperity, in the social and economic and cultural changes that transformed Rome and Italy, especially from the mid-second century BCE onwards, Rome found grounds to tear itself apart. The violence and dissensions were such that there seemed no easy escape from the cycles of destruction, and Romans of the late first century BCE looked back with nostalgia and considerable affection to the simpler days of the early Republic, when they might have been less wealthy and less successful but where times were simpler and the community more resilient and united. The last century of the Republic was a far from easy time to grow up and to negotiate one's place in the extraordinary and transforming city that was Rome.

The consequences of this turmoil for people such as Catullus cannot be overestimated. A stint as an officer in the provinces was traditionally the time for the offspring of the well-off to strengthen their credentials as Roman citizens, before immersing themselves into political life in the Roman forum or in the smaller cities and towns of Italy. Indeed, Catullus did what was expected of him; he spent almost a year (57–56) in Bithynia in the East as a member of the staff of Governor Memmius. But, as we learn from his poetry, rather than proud to be Roman, his appointment left him embittered. Close to the political centre, Catullus becomes convinced that the political infrastructure in his time is sick. Corrupt patrons, eager sycophants and the concentration of power in the hands of a small number of 'great men', such as Julius Caesar, spread ripples of discontent across the entire military and political machine, and the evident corruption of imperial government undermined Roman social values. Caught in the malfunctioning cogwheels of Roman *imperium*, Catullus represents himself as barred from the political centre and denied real involvement; as a result, he wallows in bitterness and self-doubt.

In poem 28, Catullus vents his wrath at the sycophants surrounding Piso, usually identified with Caesar's father-in-law, Calpurnius Piso Caesoninus:

> Piso's companions, worthless troops,
> equipped with little packs and ready for action,
> excellent Veranius and you, my Fabullus,
> what kind of news do you bear?
> Have you not had enough of cold and hunger following that creep?
> Do your account books show any small gain,
> on the side of costs, as do mine, who,
> having followed my praetor, I enter debt as my profit.

28.1–8

Veranius and Fabullus had featured in poem 12 (lines 14–16) as friends of the poet and key players in a circle of like-minded people. Now their small, elegant coterie has dispersed, and Veranius and Fabullus have attached themselves to Piso, eager to elicit favors and cash with flattery. The dependence of these youthful elite men on the patronage of the governor has driven them to a form of servility. Catullus' resentment has many targets in this poem. Lamenting the broken friendship (another victim of these needy times), he is as much frustrated by the political impotence of the pair as by his own losses (personal and financial). But there also lurks a deeper distress that power was concentrated in the hands of a small elite, who excluded others from power (including the son of a provincial town). Whatever the rhetoric of equality among citizens, and especially among citizens of the Italian landed elite, the concentration of power in the hands of men like Piso forced their juniors into a position of subservience. And we have not seen it all – a rather unexpected twist awaits in the second half of the poem:

> O Memmius, you've screwed me, well and for a long time –
> slowly, as I was lying on my back, with that ram of yours.
> But, as far as I can see, you two have been in an identical situation –
> stuffed by a penis just as as big …
> Seek noble friends, as they say!
> May to you two gods and goddesses bring many bad things,
> you disgraces of Romulus and Remus.

> 28.9–15

The licentiousness and aggressive sexuality of the verses has taken many critics by surprise – and caused some embarrassment. And if we were to imagine that this outburst is an eccentricity, a further look into the collection finds additional examples. Let us turn to poem 29:

> Who can watch this, and can put up with it, unless
> he's shameless and voracious and a gambler.
> Mammura having the riches that long-haired
> Gaul and remotest Britain used to have?
> Romulus, you sodomite, will you see this and allow it?
> And will he now, arrogant and extravagant,
> make a tour round everybody's bedroom,

like a white pigeon or an Adonis?
Romulus, you sodomite, will you see this and allow it?
You are shameless and voracious and a gambler.
Was it for this, you, General Unequalled,
that you have been in that remotest island of the west,
so that this fucked-out profligate of yours,
could gobble up two hundred or three hundred?
What else is this, other than perverse generosity?
Has he not been lustful or squandered enough fortune?
…
Was it for this that you have ruined everything,
most dutiful father and son-in-law of the city?

29.1–16, 23–4

Poem 29 is perhaps the most powerful of all the bitter poems in the Catullan corpus. It is a vicious attack against Mammura, who had fought alongside Pompey during the war against Mithridates in the mid-60s and then became Caesar's right-hand man during the wars in Spain, Britain and Gaul. The sexual content recalls poem 28. According to Catullus, Mamurra, a useless parasite, is taking Caesar for a ride. Mamurra becomes a predator, despoiling the provinces, eating his way across the West and through the (Italian?) fortunes he lays his hands on. But he is also a sexual predator, importuning himself into bedrooms and finding outlets for his sexual excess. Mamurra is sexually powerful, taking the sexually active part, and Romulus (who for many critics is Pompey himself) becomes a watcher, emasculated in his political sluggishness.

Adding discontent, poem 57 comes across as a wholesale condemnation for a rotten world:

They suit nicely each other, the two perverts,
passive Mamurra and passive Caesar.
And it's no wonder. Blotches equal to each other,
one from the city, the other Formian,
impressed deeply, they will stay and they will not wash away.

Equally sickly, twinned to each other,
both erudite men on a small settee.
The one no greedier an adulterer than the other,
rivals in alliance for little girls.
They suit nicely each other, the two perverts.

57.1–10

In this poem, Catullus gives up on both Caesar and Mamurra: they deserve each other. In a display of perverse political egalitarianism, the politicians are as awful as each other. And again, the main imagery is provocatively and aggressively sexual. Caesar and Mamurra are both passive, sexually dominated and penetrated. A cluster of descriptors, all insulting (*cinaedi* etc.), jostle for pride of place in this brief poem. Both Caesar and Mamurra are corrupted and emasculated in a social and political game in which they are the perverted winners.

Brought up in a world that looked back to the heyday of the Republic, Catullus watches as his hopes for Rome are violently shaken. In this world, there is no community of honours, of values and of duties in which the young and aspiring find their reward and earn respect. Instead of this nostalgic vision, Catullus and his peers find themselves screwed by their social and political superiors. The powerful dance in the bedrooms, to which they have gained access through their power, and take their pleasures where they will. Whole provinces succumb to their lusts and desires. But Catullus doesn't get his share. In a corrupt world, he desires his portion of the corrupt rewards. And those who do gain their shares (and more than their shares), the Mamurras and the Caesars, are themselves perverted and compromised in bed, much like their inferiors. Mamurra's body becomes an object of bloated disgust. Caesar and Mamurra lose all shame, but it is shame and honour that mark the Roman male.

The poems exemplify Catullus' obsession with sex and sexual violence. In Graeco-Roman culture there was a tight interconnection between gender, sexuality and power. Sexual relations were seen in a pattern of dominance and submission, control and passivity, superiority and inferiority. Borrowing the Classical Greek structures of *erastes* and *eromenos*, relationships were often understood as between lover and beloved, as the structure of the relationship slipped into Roman literature and social attitudes. This rendered the male as the dominant partner and made the female passive and inferior. Such understanding is not totally irrelevant to the modern psyche, especially in some cultures. Yet, the sexual equality and symmetry that seems to make much more sense in most contemporary societies seems to have been largely absent from the dominant sexual understanding and the sexual representations of Graeco-Roman antiquity. There were, however, exceptions. Later Greek literature, such as the Greek novel, has within it a conception that seems similar to Romantic love. Also, some later Latin literature, at least, seems aware of the possibility of a more equal relationship between lovers, especially husbands and wives. But, on the whole, Roman masculinity was heavily invested in control and domination.

Yet, power in a relationship was not just dependent on the emotional workings of the partnership: it also reflected social context. Sex inter-sected with social standing and thus there was a close relationship between masculinity, sexual activity, power and social standing. In poems such as 27, 28 and 57, political power is equated with sexual dominance. Sex is metaphoric, but in its physicality and brutality it brings home the social and political inequality in the most personal and powerful way. The sexual threat is a reflection of a manliness undermined by a loss of political influence and an inability to engage in the political arena. But that very loss of power exposes the Roman man to that sexual threat. And as we see with Caesar and Mamurra, in this game of power even the winners are perverted and thus fully exposed to sexual violation. In the world of the Late Republic, there is no escape with male integrity (and the masculine body) intact.

It is this complex interlinking between social disadvantage and threat to masculinity that explains startlingly different facets of Catullan poetry. If we continue our search of the corpus of the poet from Verona, we find that the predatory images of sexual conquest that fill Catullus with angst, exist alongside poems that offer the radical possibility of a feminised ego for the male poet. Striking amongst those is one of the most unusual poems of the collection: poem 63 describes with awe and at length Attis' entranced commitment to the cult of the great goddess Cybele. In ecstasy, Attis castrates himself. He is driven by a desire to enter the service of Cybele, a mother goddess from the East (Phrygia), whose cult had been introduced to Rome in the late third century BCE.

The poem works on many levels: dissatisfaction with his life as a youth growing up in the gymnasium feeds Attis' fascination with a foreign, Eastern cult. The exotic, effeminising character lures the boy away from the hard discipline of the gymnasium. Emasculation here is a choice, forcibly showing the need in Catullus' poetry for an alternative to the identity and destiny reserved for a (Roman) youth in the first half of the first century BCE. At the same time, the fascination with a strong female (the goddess Cybele who expects her dedicated priests to castrate themselves before presenting for duty) is celebrated. The escape from traditional masculinity is both longed for and dreaded. A great deal of the poem focuses actually on the 'morning after', when Attis recovers from his ecstasies, realises his commitment and regrets his withdrawal from the public scene.

But the lure of feminine subjectivity appears elsewhere in Catullus' poetry. Poems 61 and 62 are both choral odes, wedding hymns that juxtapose the subjectivity, expectations and life of the bride with that of the groom. Two alternative lifestyles and sensitivities are thus acknowledged, and these alternatives are presented in conflict with one another. In poem 61, Hymeneus, the marriage god, is invoked to come and support bride and groom in this transition. Though the fears of the husband are recognised, the fate of the bride seems much more ominous:

A quivering parent invokes you
on behalf of his children: for you virgins
loosen the girdle that holds their folds.

With trepidation the new husband
listens out for you with eager ear.

You yourself give up a blooming girl
from the bosom of her mother
into the hands of a fierce youth.
O Hymeneus Hymen,
O Hymen Hymeneus.

                                                      61.51–60

The female subjectivity receives more affectionate attention in poem 62. The poem starts by comparing the bride to a vine that grows infertile until she is joined by a husband elm, at which point the bride-vine begins to be tended by many farmers and oxen and starts bearing fruits. The poet warns the maiden against resistance: 'you're not to fight with a husband, maiden' (l.59). The clear implication here is the girl's aversion at the prospect of sex with her older, sturdy husband. But what is implied here is crystal clear in an earlier image:

Just as a flower that grows tucked away in a fenced garden,
unknown to the cattle, torn up by no plough,
that breezes gently stir, the sun strengthens, the rain feeds,
whom many boys and many girls desire.
But when, plucked by a sharp nail, the same flower sheds its petals,
no boys and no girls desire it.
Thus a virgin, while she stays intact, she is dear to her own,
but when the chaste flower has slipped away from a defiled body
she's neither pleasing to the boys nor dear to the girls.

                                                      62.39–48

Vivid images of yearning, beauty, loss and withdrawal from social exchanges are here woven together with sensitivity and, one feels, empathy.

We're now in the frame of mind to look at poem 11, where the poet reluctantly prepares to set off to war, sending a goodbye to his heartless girlfriend, whose brazen and promiscuous sexuality in fact likens her to the corrupt, disagreeable males of the bitter political poems we read above. What, in particular, interests us is the gender reversal and Catullus' feminised ego, as it emerges in the instructions he issues to his comrades, Furius and Aurelius, who are supposed to pass the farewell on to the girl:

> And let her not wait, as before, for my love,
> which by her fault has fallen like a flower
> on the meadow's edge having been touched
> by a passing plough.

11.21–4

Disheartened, Catullus here views his pushy girl as the plough, a symbol of penetration bringing fertility to the (feminine) earth, but also – more importantly for us here – a tool also traditionally associated with the founding or eradication of cities (in poets such as Horace and Virgil). The masculinised Lesbia thus becomes a tool in the (supposedly) civilising process of imperial expansion, which a reluctant Catullus is about to join.

Read alongside the girl-as-flower image of poem 62, Catullus (or his love) that falls on the meadow's edge in poem 11 appropriates a feminine perspective that is a far cry from the dependency, inconsistency, insecurity and other suchlike qualities traditionally associated with the female (already from Plato's *Republic*). The feminine sensibility that Catullus usurps longs, like the girl of poem 62, for independence and treasures isolation and a withdrawal from the ugly (sexual) politics of the plough. The hard, antagonistic and dominating *puella* and her (over)sensitive, side-lined lover wallowing, but secretly content, in the grief of rejection, as he treasures his unconventional status, are key markers of the new poetry of love that Catullus is inventing.

The new genre of Latin love elegy presents unconventional men making a new way in a world of a transforming Republic and the collapse of social values that comes with that transformation. In the new and uncertain world of the Late Republic, the old values are redundant and cannot be attained. All is corrupt. In response, Catullus invents a poetry of love in conscious separation from the old values. His rejection of traditional masculinity allows him to find new roles and to explore the different perspectives of the feminine. It is, of course, an empowered feminine, but the transformation of the conventional image of the virgin as flower about to be plucked into the male poet as flower about to be ploughed is a startling invention of a new masculinity. In the new world of the Late Republic, there will be new men, and elegy invents them.

The Elegists' ancestry: archaic lore and artistic experimentation in the court of kings

An elegy is written in elegiac couplets, that is an hexameter, the metre of epic poetry (a line consisting of six feet: dactyls – one long and two brief syllables – and at least one spondee – two long syllables – in the end) followed by a pentameter (i.e., a line composed of two parts, two and a half dactyls each). The truncated end of the second line – which is also cut in two in the middle – is meant to truncate, deflate and round up the message conveyed by the diptych. The metre renders the lines uneven so that it cannot reach the polished smoothness of the freer and grander epic style.

Elegiac metre has been used since Archilochus' time, in the early to mid-seventh century BCE. In the archaic and classical Greek periods, elegy, as practised by Archilochus, Theognis, Callinus, Tyrtaeus and others, often had a political and militant character which came to have an erotic content. At the end of the seventh century, Mimnermus dedicated a collection of poems to a courtesan, though the content of these poems was not directly about her. Flourishing c. 400 BCE, Antimachus of Colophon dedicated a collection of poems to his (dead) beloved as a means of commemorating her life. Nonetheless, the poems were mainly mythological stories about mythological characters; we're still a long way away from the intensely personal and involved poems of Catullus and his fellow first-century BCE Roman elegists. In between those early dedications to a beloved and the developed Roman elegiac corpus stand the Hellenistic poets with their poetic methods and innovations.

No one has been more prominently associated with Hellenistic poetry and its principles than Callimachus, a scholar working at the famous Library of Alexandria in the first half of the third century BCE. Callimachus' poetry is an eloquent sample of Alexandrian taste that encompasses a series of aesthetic and life propositions: abstaining from public duties – a prospect rather easier in a city of 300,000 people, like Alexandria, than in the relatively small classical city states – the Hellenistic poet was supposed to spend his time labouring over the details of his poetic technique. His aim was to produce sophisticated and witty poetry favouring rare and obscure themes, poetry striving for precision and elegance of form but also allusiveness and deliberate indirection, addressed to fellow connoisseurs, even though the subject matter could often be explicitly trivial and non-heroic.

In the vast, urban centres of the Hellenistic world, the role and function of epic recitals or, even more, tragic performances for the whole city was rendered meaningless; and yet, the old glory of these two genres would still attract ambitious imitators, whose ambition was more often than not matched by a lack of talent. Disengaged from their archaic aristocratic or classical civic socio-political context, the Hellenistic epics and tragedies that were produced en masse attracted the poetic wrath of Alexandrianism, which saw them as 'fat' and 'inelegant'. Though most of Callimachus' poetry unfortunately survives only in fragments, we know that he wrote, amongst other things, the *Causes* (*Aetia*), four volumes in elegiac verse of poetry explaining historical, cultural, religious, meteorological and other lore. The poems were sprinkled with wit, humour, erudition, as well as confident polemical asides and twists.

The Roman disciples

The Alexandrian taste, in general, and Callimachus' ability to produce new forms of art and embrace a new lifestyle unburdened by tradition, in particular, found imitators in Rome as early as c. 130 BCE, with poets such as Lutatius, Catulus, Porcius Licinus and Valerius Aedituus experimenting with refined epigrams. We cannot be sure how much, if anything, such poets knew of Alexandrian poetry, but Rome's expansion to the East had brought a deep engagement with Greek culture. Such contact was for Romans, like, for instance, Cato the Censor (234–149 BCE), threatening, since it undermined the *mos maiorum*, the austere ethos of the forefathers on which the glory of the Republic was felt to have been built. But a river does not turn back on its roots. A certain Parthenius from Bithynia, arrived at Rome sometime between 75 and 65 BCE, as booty from the Mithridatic Wars. He was a card-carrying Hellenistic poet and scholar able to transmit to his Roman audience Callimachus and Alexandrian theory. Parthenius worked as teacher at Rome and many a young, or not so young, mind was introduced to the new Greek poetry.

By 50 BCE, Cicero, in a letter to his friend Atticus (7.2.1), talked about a gang of emerging poets which he calls the 'newer ones' (Neoteroi), commenting unfavourably on their metric eccentricities. Cicero's impatience with these new literary coteries appears also in the *Tusculan Disputations* (3.45) where he despairs at the frivolity with which the slavish 'singers of Euphorion' (a derogatory characterisation for the Neoteroi) dismiss the traditional Roman poet Ennius. A poet and royal librarian in Antioch, Euphorion was considered to be amongst the first and most devoted followers of Callimachus.

The new poetry from the East thus gained ground in the middle decades of the first century BCE, perhaps especially outside the more establishment circles of Cicero and his friends. With the exception of Catullus, we have lost the work of the Roman New Poets. We know of Licinius Calvus, who appears to have spent an evening of poetic composition with Catullus (poem 50), Caecilius (also mentioned as fellow poet by Catullus in poem 35), Helvius Cinna and Valerius Cato. They all are supposed to have composed epyllia (little epics). This genre trumpeted its brevity as a challenge to the old-fashioned long and 'fat' epics that kept being composed.

One can read this new poetry as a poetry of withdrawal: a kind of private verse in reaction and perhaps opposition to the world of the city. Yet, there are differences between the studied scholasticism of the Alexandrians and their Roman imitators. If studious withdrawal was a perfectly accepted gesture for Callimachus, any withdrawal in the turbulent years of the Late Republic was inevitably more provocative – hence the reactions of people such as Cicero. The Neoterics received the unpressurised confidence and assertiveness of Callimachus and turned it into a political manifesto. The 'grumpy old men' of poem 5, with which we started this chapter, might mean not only the old moralists, but also the old poets. A conflict of lifestyles and beliefs emerges in this poetry, with one group looking with sadness and nostalgia to an age of lost sobriety and the *mos maiorum*, and another group who distanced themselves from the old Roman ideals and were only too keen to redirect their passion to poetry and women.

Latin love elegy emerged in Rome as a genre which, like its Hellenistic predecessors, was aesthetically refined, self-aware and affected, but it was also more militant, provocative and political. Choosing a mistress in Roman elegy meant not choosing life in the Forum, an act of defiance against the *mos maiorum* and public duty. The lover already in Catullus, but more explicitly in Tibullus, Propertius and Ovid, was a soldier of love, fighting the mistress's husband, her guardian, her nurse, or any other obstacle in the way. The military service of love shouts out that the lover is *not* a soldier fighting for Rome, as a dutiful citizen. The passion of the affair in itself was objectionable, challenging the respectable (socially-arranged) marriages of the *matronae* – the women of good families – to suitable men. Such marriages under-pinned the mythology of the Republic, and love had nothing to do with it. All along, the turbulent love lives of the poets interlaced aesthetic pleasure and artistic practice so that even the beloved ones (the *puellae*) became metaphors for poetic principles, throwing the autobiographic realism of the poetry in doubt. Poetry was as oppositional as the illicit sex and we can read the poetry as a metaphor for the sex and the sex as a metaphor for the poetry.

The subjects of Latin love elegy made very unorthodox Roman citizens: slaves to a dominating mistress, and often explicitly celebrating their slavery, they flaunted traditional social hierarchies and gendered power relations. We might say that Latin love elegy builds on a mix of registers and attitudes; a passionate tendency to frivolity and wit underlined with biting social comment. The poets were vexatious and obviously out of step yet their playfulness, wit and humour, their very elusiveness and the metaphors that, by their very nature, meant things other than the obvious meanings provided the poets a welter of ambiguity behind which to hide. Eventually, the morally conservative Augustus sent Ovid, the last of the elegists, into exile in Romania, a frosty place near the borders of the (then) known world. Augustus' regime bound itself up with a restoration of traditional values and in the world of imperial discipline elegiac playfulness and illicit but celebrated passion had no place. But first things first: before we finish this introductory overview, we need to examine some of the most striking proto-elegies by Catullus, even if not all of them were composed in the elegiac couplet.

Catullus from Verona: the poet, the soldier and the lover

The first 60 poems in the Catullan corpus are composed in iambic and lyric metres, the so-called polymetrics. The resonances with Alexandrian taste are particularly strong. Catullus paints his love affair with Lesbia in unconventional colours. We have already seen his pronounced indifference, even scorn, for the opinion of the old-fashioned minds in poem 5. Poem 7 provides a sequel:

You ask how many of your kisses
would be enough and more than enough for me, Lesbia.
As great a sum of Libyssan sand lying
in silphiophorous Cyrene
between the oracle of hot Jupiter
and ancient Battus' holy tomb,
or as many stars, when night is silent,
watch the furtive loves of men –
To kiss you with so many kisses
would more than satisfy frenzied Catullus,
and he who is prying could neither count them all out
nor ill mouth them bringing them bad luck.

7.1–12

A playful attitude colours everything in this poem. A typical erotic gesture, a request for a kiss, gives way to a self-conscious display of geographical knowledge. The topographical references are far from random: Callimachus was born in Cyrene, and claimed descent from Battus who was the founder of Cyrene. Allusively and self-consciously, Catullus signals his Alexandrian credentials, but only to those learned enough to appreciate the nod. And in amidst the geographical perambulations, Catullus inserts a covert allusion to the passion of the lovers' liaison in the reference to the sweltering oracle of Jove. The reference conjures up images of heat and lust. Playfulness and passion are to be trademarks of love elegy, and Catullus is here raising an elegiac flag for this type of emotional writing. The love of the elegists will be stolen and illicit (*furtivos amores*), to be conducted in the darkness of the night, away from the eyes of those ready to gossip.

The world of illicit love and cultivated courtesans receives fuller attention in poem 10:

Varus, my pal, took me from the Forum,
where I was passing time, to meet his love,
a little prostitute, as she seemed to me then,
but by no means unagreeable or unattractive.

10.1–4

Attractive and witty, Varus' little girlfriend cuts a distinctly Hellenistic profile. As we read more of the poem, we find that she also has good conversation; the three get talking and the girl wants to hear about Catullus' experiences in Bithynia. Sarcasm and contempt (familiar to us from the poems we read earlier) overload the response: 'Why would anyone come back richer, especially when a shit is your praetor who could not give a damn for his staff?' An attractive feature of the poem is the elaborate chummy psychology that it represents. *Meus Varus* ('my Varus') is a mate of Catullus and their friendship is built on a shared taste for an unconventional life: a life free from duties at the Forum, and spent with art and witty, elegant courtesans. The blend of lifestyle and artistic principles is obvious here and is more obvious right from the start of poem 50:

> Yesterday, Licinius, spending time during the day,
> we played a lot with my writing-tablets
> as we had agreed to be indulgent:
> each of us writing light verses
> played now with this metre, now with that,
> replying in kind to each other's jokes and toasts.
> And, yes, I left there fired up by
> your charm, Licinius, and by your wit
> …
> … wild with frenzy, I turned and tossed
> over the whole bed, longing for daylight
> so that I might talk with you and spend time with you.
>
> 50.1–8, 11–13

Catullus relives the passion of the previous evening. Only the evening was not spent in the arms of a girl. What aroused Catullus was working with his friend Licinius and the competition to outwit and impress. Cultivating their new, witty, elegant art was not only an aesthetic choice for these dilettantes: it was also a style of life they shared. Being one of the Neoteroi was a matter of writing meticulously crafted verses but also a mode of behaviour. This takes us back to poem 10 and the witty conversation of Catullus, Varus and the latter's girlfriend. Irony and teasing fill the room. In an effort to improve his standing in the eyes of the girl, Catullus lets it be known that he's come back from Bithynia with the 'local product': eight sedan bearers. The girl suspects the ploy and asks whether she could borrow them. Catullus' quick exit involves another studied trope: the bearers are shared between him and Cinna (another known New Poet); these kindred spirits share not only artistic advice but also accessories – one presumes also girls – in a concerted effort to appear cool and successful, socially as well as artistically. But the pretension is seen through by the girl: the *puella* not only partakes in the conversation, but she has the upper hand.

Such frivolous episodes are juxtaposed with more sombre reflections on the futility and fickleness of love. Famous among the latter is poem 8, the first admission of rejection by the harsh mistress. Many more rejections will follow in the Catullan corpus – and in the elegiac corpus, as we shall see.

> Poor Catullus, you should stop being absurd
> and you must consider lost what you see has been lost.
> Bright sunshine shone for you, at one time,
> when you kept going where your girl would lead.
> …
> Now she does not want, and you must not want, you feeble.
> And you must neither chase her who runs away nor live in misery.
> But with a firm mind be steadfast.
> Goodbye girl. Catullus now stands firm.
>
> 8.1–4, 9–12

And so on and so forth. The rest of the poem is an admonition by Catullus to himself to show even temper, reject the unstable passions of the heart and snap out of his misery at the rejection of the fickle *puella*. In fact, the whole poem is a balance between two opposing wills: the girl's and the rejected poet's. The poet makes a decision to break away from the girl, break from the habit of letting her making decisions about them. There is a power struggle going on. The poem concludes indecisively: Catullus is unable to retrieve his independence (and thus his masculine authority), able only to prevaricate in broody rumination suspended between two untenable positions. In fact, he seems always drawn back to the relationship that is so central to his poetry and to the manufacturing of the self that is so central to that poetry. Whatever he tries, he is enslaved.

In poem 11, which we saw above, he actually appears to have the strength to break from the girl. Bidding farewell to another two of his mates, he has a special request for Furius and Aurelius :

> Deliver to my girl a few harsh words:
> may she live and prosper with her debauchers
> all three hundred she holds together in her embrace,
> Loving none truly but again and again
> bringing them all to a climax ...

> 11.15–20

And yet, when we reach the epigrams (i.e. poems 65–116, written in elegiac metre) he is trapped still in an elegiac mourning in which the relationship becomes nostalgic; this liminality (being neither one thing nor the other) has become totally unbearable. Turning to poem 72, we are immediately struck by a new language, a new vocabulary:

> You said once, Lesbia, that you alone knew Catullus,
> and that you did not wish to have not even Jove before me.
> I loved you then, not only as a commoner would love their girl,
> but as a father loves his sons and sons-in-law.

> 72.1–4

The choice of terms is striking. Catullus would like us to believe that the quality of his erstwhile love for Lesbia can be compared to the filial love of a man for his offspring by blood and by marriage. Familial ties are invoked to describe feelings that in poems like 5 or 7, that we saw above, were explicitly scornful of any traditional forms of bonding, whether pertaining to the family, or the wider society alike. We will find parallels in poem 76:

If there is any satisfaction for a man recalling former kindnesses,
when a man reflects that he has been true
and has neither broken a solemn promise nor in any pact
abused the gods' will to deceive his fellow men,
then much happiness awaits ready for you, Catullus,
well into your old age, from this ungrateful love.

76.1–6

In poem 76 (as in poem 72) Catullus dresses his love for Lesbia in the language of the aristocratic ties of *amicitia*, the bonds of honourable friendship that held together the Roman citizenry. In the Latin original, the words used are unmistakeably official and political: *officium* (responsibility) in poem 72; *benefacta* (favours), *fides* (honesty/pledge), *foedus* (charter/treaty) in poem 76.

Catullus innovatively has transposed the language of *amicitia* to the realm of illicit, unconventional love. Yet, the effect is odd. Rather than subverting the language of power and public life, the language alienates Catullus. His duties are to the mistress. His treaty is with the mistress. He attempts to see a family and new sons in the mistress. Catullus plays the conventional Roman, but in a radically unconventional context. What we witness is a deep isolation emerging as a result of the paradoxes of the relationship. How could Catullus take pleasure from Lesbia's ungrateful love, as he hopes to do in 76? Lesbia is not bound by the honour of Roman friendship. Lesbia is not going to reciprocate, honouring his devotion, and so Catullus is condemned to an impossible situation: to not like her and yet to love, as we are told in poem 75, echoing the poignant and infamous poem 85:

I hate and I love. Why do I do that, you might ask.
I do not know, but I feel it happening, and am tortured.

And poem 87 summarises pithily this insurmountable impass: 'no faith so great was ever found in any contract, as has been found in my part of loving you.'

No contract of friendship has ever been attended with more

faithfulness. What we get from these poems is only the one part of the equation and equivalence that traditionally accommodated *amicitia*. Catullus' agonising last attempt to exchange the identity of the love with that of the Roman gentleman rings hollow. There is no society of friends for Catullus: his own choices have led to self-exclusion from those worlds of binding reciprocity and to a wild attempt to reinvent that world in his relationship to his mistress. The sheer impossibility of that attempt seems to defy all logic. In fact, that honourable society is disintegrating, as we saw in his angry poems about corrupt patronage. Catullus' love for Lesbia is not *amicitia*; if anything, it lays invidious claims to another man's property, the husband's, assaulting the fundamental bonds of *amicitia*. Catullus is left alone and disconsolate, hating and loving, but without the easy guide of a moral code. He has invested all his identity in a relationship with an ideal of a woman, but that ideal has turned out to be real and rebellious. The real of sex, with a real woman, trumps the ideal of poetry.

Poem 76 deserves special attention as an example of protoelegy. Epigrammatic brevity and a liking for a final twist are combined with a more expanded narrative, though much of the story is alluded to or implied. This narrative form of love will become typical of the elegiac corpus. An unrequited lover suffers at the hands of an ungrateful *puella*. He is sad and he is angry. He would like to fight for the *puella* but also has to admit the futility of such a struggle. The quintessential elements of Latin love elegy are all present. Present also in Catullus is a deep bitterness at an exclusion from society, desired, even provoked, and yet always vexing. In this sense, Lesbia remains unresolved in the poems. She is the creation of the poet through whom the poet as personality is also created. But as with Varro's girl, she had a kick in her, a wit which makes her do the unexpected and reverse the relationship between poet and lover. As the poet explores his subservience to the mistress and in so doing reverses many of the conventional values of Roman society, he begins to construct an alternative universe of moral values. In those moral values, Catullus imagines that he can find peace with Lesbia. He can construct his treaty and live his family life. But

Lesbia is better than that. She is never his to control. She is always threatening and unconventional. Catullus' dream world is kicked over. In the conflicting emotions of the Catullan corpus, there is no easy answer. The new masculinity finds making sense of the world no easier than the old masculinity did. As the Republic spins into the Empire and the Roman revolution takes a further hold, so elegy develops and explores the continued paradoxes and failures of the elegiac persona. And always, lying behind these explorations, is the original *puella*, Catullus' irrepressible, oft-kissed and innumerate Lesbia.

2

Dream and Desire: Tibullus at a Crossroads

Approximately 25 to 30 years separate Catullus from the 'eldest' of the Latin elegists: Albius Tibullus is said to have been born c. 60–55 BCE in Pedum, east of Rome, and, like Catullus, Propertius and Ovid, he belonged to the equestrian class. If in Catullus' lifetime the Roman Republic was breathing its last, overwhelmed by continuous war between overambitious generals, Tibullus' life was marked by the last of these civil wars (between Octavian and Mark Antony), but also, importantly, by the gradual but irrevocable concentration of power in the hands of Octavian and the political consequences of this shift. And yet, their respective poetic corpora could not be further apart in terms of tone. Catullus' rude anger and pent-up frustration is all but gone in Tibullus' poetry. Instead, a soft and gentle tone seems to flow through the collection. Tibullus' poems are almost polite complaints; the tone is tactful with a pervasive sense of loss expressed in wistful melancholy and gentle recollection, most of the time.

In many ways Catullus and Tibullus look at the same world – but from different angles, and so they see different things. Being part of the old world, Catullus can share the angst of it falling to pieces; Tibullus is more distant and less vulnerable to angry Catullan grief, but he is also enmeshed in the emerging fabric of the new world; he is part of the process of that world's creation, an involved party and not a passive spectator. There is still much at stake, socially and politically, for Tibullus, as there was for Catullus. For all the restored freedoms that Octavian claimed to be defending and renewing, this was a world that Tibullus could hardly recognise. Tibullus was still expected to train in rhetoric, have a stint at the frontier, and become a career politician, but he was still dislocated in this society. Unlike Catullus, he chose to deal with his lurking dissatisfaction through melancholic introspection which manifested itself in an earnest attempt at withdrawal from the socio-political sphere. Such withdrawal was not without cost and, as with Catullus' alienation from the world of politics, it could cause enormous strain to the self-image of elite Roman males, shocked not to find their 'rightful' place in their own city.

The differences become crystal clear if we juxtapose the ranting political discourse on display in Catullus' poetry, as explored in Chapter 1, with the virtual absence of references to Octavian in the Tibullan corpus. As we are going to see, Tibullus worries a great deal about his Roman identity and his role in this emergent world of Octavian's making. In this sense, he is much more enmeshed in the politics of his time than his fellow elegists (Propertius and Ovid) will be. The debate on what it is to be a Roman citizen is still open-ended in Tibullus' time and lingers throughout his poetry. By the time of Propertius and, certainly, Ovid, the concentration of power in the hands of Octavian, who, contrary to some later views, displayed his power in monuments, ceremonials and coinage (the mass media of antiquity), rendered much of this discussion irrelevant and we will address these issues in the chapters that follow. There is in Tibullus' poems a puzzling, intriguing quality: a studied air of distance from the political centre and yet a constant and deep-seated preoccupation with Roman duties, manhood and citizenship. Even Tibullus' patron, one of his most explicit links to the establishment, shares this ambivalence: Messalla Corvinus was an influential politician, who concentrated a circle of poets and artists around him and took young Tibullus under his wings. He was a trusted member of the Augustan circle and was made Prefect of the City when Augustus left for military duties in the provinces. Yet, Messalla was also sensitive to the views and opinions of his fellow senators, who pressurised him to resign his post. Messalla's position was different to the other famous patron of arts, Maecenas, a close colleague and supporter of Octavian, whose political and social position depended very much on his closeness to the Augustan court. Whereas Maecenas remained very much a court politician, Messalla campaigned in Acquitania on behalf of Octavian (and possibly elsewhere) and was one of the last Romans not from the imperial family ever to be awarded the great distinction of a triumphal procession through the streets of Rome. Messalla existed between the old senatorial politics and the new imperial court.

A quality that sets Tibullus' text apart from the other elegists is its dreamlike, low-key tone, a tenderness and even meekness foreign to Propertius with his frequent exaggerated outbursts and to Ovid with his biting, if witty, criticism. Though Quintilian, the Spaniard orator and teacher who flourished in Rome of the late first century BCE, famously called Tibullus 'polished and elegant' (*tersus atque elegans*) and favoured him above Propertius (*Institutio Oratoria* 10.1.93), Tibullus had not caught the eye of modern critics, until very recently. Critics have tended to be nonplussed by his reluctance to assert, his laid-back style and guarded, introspective voice. Expecting vigour and narrative jolts that would provoke and shake the establishment (a technique favoured by both Propertius and Ovid, and indeed Catullus), critics would be faced with Tibullus' constant repetitions, contradictions, regressions and a certain reticent inarticulacy, in all of which they saw lack of spirit and skill. Contemporary readers, however, accustomed to more flexible (and less linear) modes of narrative, have been more appreciative of the overall effects of repetition and contradiction in Tibullus' poetry. His perceived inarticulacy has prompted scholars to probe the unresolved tensions pervading the corpus. Nowadays, Tibullus is seen as a subtle juggler of contrasting emotions and desires, equipped with a generosity of spirit and a quiet determination to face the impossible dilemmas of Rome at this moment of profound change.

Three books have come down to us in the *Corpus Tibullianum*. The first two belong to Tibullus. The third book offers us an assortment of poems believed to have been written by people associated with Messalla. The most important poems in this book are 3.13 to 3.18: these are poems written by Sulpicia, the only woman Latin poet whose work is today extant. We will talk separately about Sulpicia:

she is too important to tuck away! Here we concentrate on the first
two books of the collection, and especially Book One, where the main
concerns and loves in Tibullus' poetry jostle for a place, mingling
but often disturbing, or competing with, each other. The paramount
dream of Tibullus' poetry and life is a peaceful, simple existence in the
countryside. There will be no riches in his farmland; happy poverty
and leisure will suffice, as long as a fire is lit in the humble hearth. This
dream dominates his images and feelings throughout the collection: an
Arcadia Tibullus will never quite attain and which always haunts him.
Two figures loom in his poetry: Messalla, his patron and friend whom
Tibullus wants at his side, and Delia, his girlfriend, a rich man's wife,
invited by Tibullus to rest in his embrace and share his humble country
life. The question is: will Messalla try to wrench Tibullus away from his
leisurely abode and into the harsh life of a military man? And how will
Delia, the rich man's spouse, adjust to the sparseness of the farm life
of Tibullan fantasy? The rest of the chapter will explore these pressures
in Tibullus' world. In the process, many questions and incongruities
will surface: facing the improbable seems to be Tibullus' own powerful
twist, a gesture of bravery and folly under the cover of his unassuming
and unprepossessing verse.

The collection opens with the dream:

Let someone else amass wealth for themselves in bright gold
and occupy many acres of cultivated land –
Let him spend frightful days of service, with the enemy at his doorstep,
while the blare of the trumpets chase his sleep away.
But let my poverty lead me to sluggish life,
as long as fire perpetually illuminates my hearth.

1.1.1–6

The next 20 or so lines continue with this reverie of contentment in
poverty, as Tibullus indulges in his farm duties: he will be tending
the vines with an experienced hand early in the season, expecting
abundant produce, and giving back thankfully and generously to the
gods, a gesture for their support and protection. The poet brims with

happiness and hope as he addresses Ceres, Priapus and the Lares (divinities of crops, fertility and the household) with promises of the gifts that all will receive, even though his lands have been diminished (as a result of confiscations that took place after the Battle of Philippi in 42 BCE).

But come line 25 and the bliss is dispersed:

If only I could now live contently with little
and not be given to the never-ending road,
but avoid the heat of the Dog-star's summer rising,
under the shadow of a tree, beside the running waters of a stream.

1.1.25–8

With the sudden jolt back, Tibullus' identity is revealed. He is a soldier, in the service of Rome, bound to be asked to uproot and hit the road. His reluctance is hardly concealed: this is not how Tibullus would choose to spend his life; if it were up to him, he would recline under a tree by a brook, dodging the intense heat of the July days after the onset of Sirius. For the knowledgeable readers of the first century BCE, the last two lines of the above quote constitute an unmissable literary reference. Resting under the thick shade of a tree in the afternoon heat was also the favourite pastime of the Arcadian and unreal shepherds of Virgil's *Eclogues*, published c. 36 BCE, ten or so years earlier. We will not get into the details of the Virgilian collection, but the influence permeates Tibullus' poetry and as the door into the pastoral world creaks open, we can hardly avoid thinking about Virgil as well as Tibullus. Virgilian pastoral displays a simplicity, humility, gentle affection for the community, and heightened sensitivity to the frailty and innocence of life. This subtle world is threatened by the clamour of military life that Tibullus, the soldier, has to endure.

Though shaken by the recollection of the prospect of military service, Tibullus makes a valiant attempt to pull himself away from the unpleasant associations and return to his dream of safe, unassuming poverty:

I do not ask for the riches and rewards of my fathers
and all that that seasoned harvest brought to my ancient ancestors.
A small field is enough, enough is reposing in a bed
and resting my limbs on a familiar couch.
What a pleasure to hear the harsh winds,
as I lie there holding my girl in a tender embace.

1.1.41–6

Poverty and the girl in his arms: the perfect combination for Tibullus,
who nevertheless cannot quite lay the ghost of war to rest:

O let all the gold and yet more emerald perish
sooner than any girl might weep for my marching away.

51–2

War and military campaigns cause grief to the lovers and make the
mistress weep. So, continues Tibullus, it is all right for Messalla to
undertake expeditions to far away lands. He himself, however, has a
different duty to perform and a different hardship to endure:

The chains of a beautiful girl hold me prisoner
and at her cruel door I sit as porter.

55–6

Love is opposed to war and this is a natural opposition in Tibullus'
poems: love affairs and mistresses belong with Tibullus' retreat, tucked
away in his embrace in front of the glowing fire, and this retreat is
secured by renouncing the military life and the riches that come with
it. And yet, something jars in the above description: the poet/farmer is
not simply in love; he is captive, held prisoner at his girl's cruel door.
The rural freedom of Tibullus' dream is disturbingly revised. Is the
blissful love actually a form of captivity for the lover? And why is the
girl's door cruel?

However sudden, this abrupt transition from unforced contentment
to incarceration lands us in one of the main themes (*topoi*) of the
elegiac genre: *servitia amoris*, the slavery of love. Love in Latin elegy is

a constant hunt, a pursuit of a reluctant, harsh girl (*dura puella*) who does not think that her suitor is worthy of her affections. In a direct inversion of Roman gender stereotypes, the pursuing lover responds to his girl's harshness with weak compliance: he'll do anything to get the girl; she is the mistress and he is her slave prepared to plead outside her firmly locked door (another major elegiac *topos*: the excluded lover, *exclusus amator*). In this fictional world, the traditionally dominant (male) has swapped places with the traditionally obedient (female) in a provocative non-compliance with social norms.

Considerable energy has gone into understanding this willed inversion and its socio-political consequences. For all its fictional character, the construct of the elegiac *puella* is rendered more historical when one takes into account the emergence in the literature of the Late Republic of independent, literate and powerful women, such as Cornelia, the mother of Gracchi; Hortensia, who led female protests against the triumvirs; Clodia, the scandalous sister of the equally scandalous popular politician Clodius; and the various powerful wives of Mark Antony. The legendary feminine values of the foundational myths of Rome – modesty, chastity, discipline, and so on – that sustained stories such as that of virtuous, raped Lucretia, came under pressure in a world of cultural change and accumulation of wealth. As the respectable Roman women's presence, presentation and responsibilities became more significant for their men's position in society, the education of elite women became a requirement. Alongside the respectable world of *matronae* and their marriages of political expedience, a new world flourished in the first century BCE: a demi-monde, the world of cultivated courtesans entertaining the husbands of the upper class outside wedlock, with witty company, erudite conversation, and sex. Yet, it seems that elite women could also move within this demi-monde, finding love and romantic liaisons outside the confines of marriage, willing participants in a world of new social rules.

Read against this social background, Tibullus' change of mood brings him in line with Propertius and Ovid, and with what we now perceive to be the recognisable formulaic features of the elegiac genre.

Tibullus' play with captivity will be repeated in his poetry. In poem 1.6.37–8, he pleads with Eros, the god of Love, to grant him permission to serve her at all costs: 'But let me be her slave. You could flog me when it pleases you or reign me with chains and I'll take my punishment.' In Book Two, Delia has disappeared to be replaced by a harsh and heartless mistress, with an appropriate name: Nemesis (Revenge). Next to Nemesis, Delia might start seeming more like a high school sweetheart. Nemesis is calculating, ruthless and keen only on money. In his dedicated poverty (another typical elegiac mode), Tibullus has nothing to offer to Nemesis, and, indeed, the whole book is replete with images of the humiliation and degradation of the scorned lover. And yet, poem 2.4 contains a fervent acceptance of the role of the slave-to-love, despite the feelings of despondency and disappointment:

> Here I see slavery and a mistress waiting for me.
> Farewell now to the freedom of my forefathers.
> Sad slavery is offered to me – I am held in chains
> and Love never relaxes the bonds for me, the wretched one.

> 2.4.1–4

Equally, the fleeting image of him standing in front of the shut and cruel door of the unyielding girl – which we witnessed in 1.1.55–6 – receives a fuller treatment in 1.2. Whether actually delivered in front of a door, or soliloquised at home, or a part of a reverie (all such possibilities have been considered), this long elegy dramatises the *topos* of the excluded lover with wit and ingenuity. The husband as enemy is dully dominant, and a witch is deployed in the hope that her magic skills will assist the lover with his cunning plan:

> She has composed a spell for me that you can use to deceive.
> Sing it out loud thrice and spit thrice after you have spoken the words,
> and then he will not be able to believe anything from anyone about us,
> not even himself, if he see us with his own eyes in your soft bed.

> 1.2.55–8

* * *

As we will have the chance to explore with Propertius and Ovid, the elegiac corpus is scattered with countless reworkings of all the above *topoi*. The locked out lover, the slave lover, the poor lover, the guardian/ husband, love as cunning and deceit, bawds and witches will all feature in abundance in the other two elegists. One is justified in feeling that a great deal of elegy is about an erudite competition in innovative yet recognisable tropes of amatory communication. One might say that this literary race to outwit each other may be partly responsible for the quick burn-out of the genre (all possibilities spent), but this process is much more complex. However, if the recurrence of formulaic tropes and modes wins Tibullus an entry ticket to the elegiac club and allows us to see a certain consistency between him and his fellow elegists, it cannot also conceal the many contradictions and inconsistencies in the Tibullan corpus. These incongruities make Tibullus stand apart from the others and explain a lot about the uneven development of the genre. We will thus spend the rest of this chapter in an attempt to map them out.

Let us recall Tibullus' ideal life in the country. Tibullus wishes to withdraw into a peaceful life of serenity and inaction, under the shade of a thick tree during the sleepy hours of a summer afternoon. Midday heat and stillness, cool running waters, leisurely inaction, all point, as already mentioned, to another genre, Virgilian pastoral, also renowned for its subtle and refined worldview and jealous protection of its boundaries from the invasion of the turbulent world of politics. A particular phrase in the initial six lines of Tibullus' dream deserves special attention: inert life (*vitae inerti*, 1.1.5). Tibullus hopes that his withdrawal and resulting poverty will gain him a place in a world devoid of strain and action. The foregrounding of inaction recalls images of a lost Golden Age; indeed, within a couple of poems we come across an expressed nostalgia for the bygone times of perfection:

How well they used to live during the reign of Saturn, before
the land was opened to long roads.

The pine had not yet looked down on the dark blue waves
or provided the winds with full sails.
And no wandering seaman seeking profit in unfamiliar lands
had yet loaded his ship with foreign goods.
Those days, the strong bull had not yet yielded to the yoke
and the horse did not chew the bit with tamed mouth.
No houses had doors. No fixed stone stood on the fields
to rule the land with indisputable boundaries.
The oak trees gave honey, and the sheep would offer
willingly their easy flowing milk to the untroubled men.
Armies and anger and war were not yet known.
The cruel blacksmiths had not yet forged the sword with cruel art.

1.3.35–48

The apparatus of a Golden Age is here present. The pine planks of boats did not criss-cross the seas, in a direct allusion to the presentation of the Golden Age in another landmark neoteric poem, Catullus 64. Unshepherded sheep offer milk in plenitude to carefree people and honey runs freely down the bark of trees (in yet further direct references to more neoteric stock: Virgil's *4th Eclogue*). Land, people and animal live in unhurried harmony and instinctive cooperation.

Literary nostalgia for a carefree Arcadia reigns in this passage. But when prompted to think on the details of his dreamland, Tibullus imagines work, timely and meticulous. Is he the leisurely shepherd poet of the *Eclogues*? Or the hard working, patient farmer of the *Georgics*, imbued with Octavian's new emphasis on simplicity of life and hard work on land? Lines 1.1.7–8 would rather suggest the second:

I would plant the tender vines at the right time,
and, myself a peasant, the tall fruit trees with skilful hand.

Further down, the coarse, austere life in contented labour is once again welcome:

Nor that I would be ashamed to wield a hoe from time to time
or rebuke the slow oxen with a goad,

nor would it be irksome for me to bring home a ewe lamb in my arms
or a young goat abandoned by a forgetful mother.

1.1.29–32

The shift from a leisurely, sophisticated nostalgia for merry Arcadia
to the unadorned realities of everyday farming is unmistakeable and
somewhat confusing. Tibullus may explicitly be wishing to avoid
service in the army, but Octavian could not but be pleased with the
traditional Roman rustic morality propagated by Tibullus in this model
of a hard-working, experienced farmer. It is exactly such farmers who
were imagined as the backbone of Rome's legions. Emerging from
his dreamland, engaging with new and austere conservatism of the
imperial regime, Tibullus projects a mixed image of a sophisticated
new poet keen to adjust to the demands of his leader and put himself
in the service of Rome.

The purity of the dream countryside, Tibullus' Arcadia, is
undermined almost at the same time as it is introduced. Arcadia
stands apart from the concerns of real time and the limitations of
history, and in the hands of the pastoral poet Theocritus, a rough
contemporary and kindred spirit of Callimachus, became a symbol
of Hellenistic art and spirit. However, in the Latin texts of the first
century BCE, Arcadia is under siege. It does not escape real time
or the constraints of history; it continuously competes with Rome
and its demands. Political strife and edicts invade the boundaries of
Arcadia; Virgilian pastoral derives much of its lingering melancholy
from the fragility of its community.

The same fragility undermines Tibullus' vision. The sweet and soft
tones are punctuated by gnawing uncertainty. Delia, in poem 1.2,
torments Tibullus and disturbs his blissful dream of a countryside
love that he conjured up in poem 1.1.43–6. The gentle hues of life
in the country are here replaced by the inhospitable dark step of the
puella's closed door. The poet-cum-excluded lover enlists all his wits
(and the help of a witch) to devise ways for him and Delia to elude the
attentions of the latter's husband. But his faith in his plan and in his

puella suddenly falters: 'The same witch even promised, though I find it hard to believe, by her spells or herbs to liberate me from my love' (1.2.61–2). The witch has offered the unthinkable: to free Tibullus of his love, plunging him into deep confusion. 'I desired for love to be shared, not altogether absent. How could I ever wish to live without you?' he responds in bewilderment (1.2.65–6). Tibullus may wonder at the witch's suggestion, but the impossible has been uttered: would Tibullus be better off without his love? Is his love so harmful that he needs rescuing? Why might that be so? Is Delia simply not returning the poet's love? Or is she a figure incompatible to the pastoral serenity of Tibullus daydreams?

The questions are not bound to be answered within either Book One or Book Two of the Tibullan corpus. In fact, as the poems progress, yet new obstacles to the country life emerge, undermining further the apparent assurance with which the dream had initially been presented. Poem 1.3 deals with perhaps the most puzzling of those obstacles: Messalla, his patron, friend and leader. It is in this poem that all the incompatibilities that fester within Tibullus' vision come to the surface. The poem, written soon after the Battle of Actium in 31 BCE, begins with Tibullus ill, and regretting the illness that forced him to stay captive on the island of Phaeacia, unable to follow his leader and friend to the East (1.3.1–11). Tibullus' many identities here blend effortlessly, it seems, but also confusingly. Tibullus laments the illness that prevents him from fulfilling his duties as a Roman citizen. And yet, once bed-ridden, his thoughts turn to Delia, and her grief over his departure with Messalla. We are thus reminded of his role as a lover, clearly incompatible with his duty as a soldier (1.3.11–22). If it were up to her, Delia would keep Tibullus back from the war; and Messalla makes Delia cry by taking her beloved away. Faced with the incompatible demands of patron and lover, Tibullus escapes both and breaks into a reverie of Golden Age, the image we studied above (1.3.35–48). He then writes his own epitaph, the epitaph of a soldier, where Messalla gets a mention but Delia does not:

Here lies Tibullus wasted by inexorable death
while following Messalla through land and through sea.

1.3.55–6

The next image takes us to the Elysian fields, but somewhat changed: this is not the traditional place of rest for the heroes; lovers inhabit this blissful realm with Venus as the leader of the souls in the place of Hermes:

But me, as I have always been courteous to tender love,
Venus herself will lead to the Elysian fields.
There songs and dances flourish, and flitting everywhere
the birds sing with slender throat their tender tunes.
Uncultivated land bears cassia and over all the fields
bounteous land flowers with scented roses.

1.3.57–62

A blend of the imagery traditionally associated with the Elysian fields, and a landscape brimming with art, brings us back to pastoral poetics. So Tibullus edges back into his dream of countryside life away from time and history. But the next few lines complicate his retreat:

But ranks of young men mixed with tender girls play together,
and Love stirs his battles continuously.
There are those to whom grabby Death came while they were in love
and their hair is adorned by myrtle wreath for all to see.

1.3.63–6

The young men and women in this uplifting reverie may be lovers, but they are also soldiers, engaged in battles of love. Here lovers cannot be shepherds; love is war and the intensity of passion drives them away from Arcadia and its gentle rhythm of life. At the end of the passage, they are victors in a military procession, a triumph, with myrtle wreaths on their head, successful in love but torn away from the timeless, fantasy world, to become part of the Roman machinery of war again. The rest of the poem simply makes sure that we are robbed of any certainty as to what Tibullus experiences or believes. The last part of the narrative is Tibullus begging Delia to be faithful and a prayer, perhaps just a desire, for an uncomplicated, devoted life next to his ever absent girl (1.3.83–94).

The tension between countryside, Delia and his citizen duties continues in 1.7. The poem is a eulogy written for Messalla's birthday, his first after his triumph in 27 BCE. It starts seemingly determined to pay tribute to Roman success.

> Our Roman people have seen
> new triumphs, and defeated leader with arms in captivity's chains,
> and you, Messalla, bearing the conquering laurel,   ·
> an ivory chariot was carrying, drawn by shiny horses.
>
> 1.7.5–8

Unlike in poem 1.3, when Tibullus was detained by illness, here he is an integral part of Roman history and ceremony. 'Not without me was your esteem acquired' (1.7.9). He enumerates the various victories they together attained, the general and his soldier. But then ambivalence creeps in: 'or shall I sing of Cydnus … or Taurus … Why tell of white doves flying … how the towers of Tyre … look over the vast sea …' (1.7.13–22). So it was not the relationship between a general and a soldier that brings Tibullus to the triumph: he is part of the Roman triumphs because he can sing of them, a poet in cordial relationship with his patron. With his poetic hat on, though, Tibullus does not only sing of wars; in fact, he more often does *not* sing of wars, busy with serving the god of Love and a mistress. And Messalla is invited into this amatory world. In 1.5, Tibullus dreams of a lucky life (*felicem vitam*):

> 'I tend the farm' I thought 'and Delia will be there to guard the grain
> while the harvest is threshed on the floor baking in the hot sun.
> Or she will look after the grapes for me in the full troughs
> And the white must newly pressed by swift feet.
> …
> Here my Messalla will come, and for him Delia will pick
> sweet apples from our best trees,

and, honouring his greatness, she will attend to every need of his,
prepare a banquet for him and serve it to him herself.'

1.5.21–4, 31–4

Messalla is affectionately invited into the rural idyll, a great Roman
general in the midst of the indolent world of the countryside. And yet,
this rural idyll fits naturally with the austere, hard-working world of
Virgil's *Georgics*, in which Messalla may not be such an incongruous
figure. Virgil himself was content (or daring enough) to include a
triumphant Caesar in his own luscious idyll, building for him a shrine
in the green meadows close to where the river Mincius' water flows
zigzagging along the bank reeds (*Georgics* 3.13–16).

The somewhat surprising balance of all of Tibullus' different attrac-
tions is, however, short-lived. In poem 1.6, Tibullus is again wracked by
doubt and suspicion for his heartless girlfriend, who may be deceiving
him as well as her husband. And Book Two, with a new mistress,
Nemesis, is replete with the humiliations of the poet-lover. The rural
harmony is destroyed for good, making permanent the rift between
elegy and pastoral.

In fact, this tension between elegiac and pastoral worlds in the
Tibullan corpus is not new: we are told in Virgil's *Eclogues* 10 that
Gallus, new poet/political man/wounded lover, flirted with the serenity
and comfort of Arcadia. The whole landscape was his friend and affec-
tionately called him to partake into its comforts. Gallus is tempted, but
in the end he cannot abandon his unrequited passion for Lycoris, and
such passion cannot be accommodated in the gentle pastoral world.
Tibullus in his poetry has placed himself in the exact reverse position
to Gallus: he has conjured up a dream of gentle life in the countryside,
a retreat from the alarming uncertainties that Roman life in the
Forum and on the frontiers inflicted upon even the 'party faithful' in
the mid-first century BCE. Messalla is invited into this rural idyll as
a friend, but he is also the man who built the road from city to town
(1.7.57–62). Tibullus can no longer barricade into his dream: the road
takes him out to new campaigns with Messalla.

Tibullus has also conjured up gentle love in the countryside: he has imagined Delia by his deathbed and then at his funeral (1.1.57–68). Even at his funeral, he is hoping for gentle affection rather than distraught and distressing outbursts of grief: 'Do not hurt my shade, Delia: spare your flowing hair and your tender cheeks' (1.1.67–8). But the subtle emotion that Tibullus searches for is violated by the intensities of love elegy. Book One does not finish with an image of content affection, as it started (1.1.45–6), but with the harsh, disturbing and decidedly unelegaic image of a wife-beating farmer:

> The countryman drives home from the grove
> hardly sober himself, wife and children in the wagon.
> Then Venus' battle flares up. And then the woman
> laments torn hair and broken door.
> Bruised she weeps for her tender cheeks but the winner also weeps
> that his mad hands were so strong.
> But impudent Love feeds the quarrel with evil words
> and sits there, slow to be moved, between the furious pair.
>
> 1.10.51–8

This is perhaps the closest to an explicit admission that Tibullus, the lover, will never find peace in his dreamy countryside and that the idyll of the countryside can be brutal: a scene of domestic violence rather than mutual elegiac love. Both the farmer and his wife feel sorry for the strife between them, but, as Ovid will tell us wisely, Love conquers all, and so forces all parties to succumb to his whim. Whichever way one looks at it, Tibullus provides an ineffective model of new manhood in these turbulent and unresolved times. The dream of the country cannot survive the road to the city.

Coda: Sulpicia

No study of the Roman elegiac voice could ignore Sulpicia, a female poet whose lines and love take the reader aback. The elegies are unconventional. They were preserved through the Middle Ages, tucked away inside the third book of the *Corpus Tibullianum*. Unlike the first two books of the corpus, which were written by Tibullus, the third book of the *Corpus* is a miscellany of poems. Poems 3.1 to 3.6 are attributed to a certain Lygdamus. Poems 3.8 to 3.12 are about Sulpicia's love for Cerinthus. The group of poems that has attracted most controversy are 3.13–3.18, poems attributed to Sulpicia herself. Not very much is known about Sulpicia. Most significantly, she was the niece of Messala, Tibullus' and other poets' patron. An upper-class, educated young woman, Sulpicia took (mostly male) critics and readers by surprise. Up until the last third of the twentieth century, her poems were regarded as artless, unsophisticated ruminations or at best romantic outbursts of an adolescent girl. But recently, more sensitive and imaginative readings have re-evaluated these gems. We are now well aware of the technical proficiency and exactitude of Sulpicia's elegiac couplets. The brevity of her poems place her within a Hellenistic tradition of the amatory epigram while the robustness of her narrative associates her closely with the personal poetry of the elegists. She is a bit like Tibullus, in her more sensitive moments, but she also reminds us of Propertius in the vehemence of her feelings. Yet, she is never far from the Ovidian style, in her ability to flout convention, and her yearning for freedom bears a strong resemblance to the early poems of Catullus (see especially poems 5 and 7) with his own celebration of the power of limitless love to defy and annoy the loveless, joyless seniors.

Poem 3.13 (the first of Sulpicia's own poems) is both alluring and hard to place:

> Such love has come that there would be more talk about it
> if I hid it than if I laid it bare for all to see.
> Persuaded by my poetry Venus Cytherea
> brought him and placed him in my arms.
> Venus has fulfilled in full her vow. Let my joy be talked about
> let it be discussed by those who have no joys of their own.
> I would not wish to order my messages to be sealed
> so no one could read them before my lover.

It pleases me to sin: and it tires me to wear a mask to preserve
good reputation. The world shall say I have found my match.

3.13.1–13

Unlike Ovid, who takes pleasure in staging secrecy and orchestrating
deceit (of husbands, escorts and any other who might stand in the way
of the two lovers), Sulpicia dispenses with artifice altogether. She is
confident in her art, both poetic and amatory. Spontaneity goes hand in
hand with calculation and elaborateness of style (as the original Latin
suggests to us), giving us a poet like no one else in her milieu. Sulpicia
adopts a number of roles all at once, and not all of them are mutually
compatible. Her trained verse and strong narrative belong to the best
traditions of Roman elegiac poetry, fully mindful of the debts owed to
Hellenistic principles of refinement and sophistications. Poems 3.14
and 3.15, however, place Sulpicia in a situation we associate with the
puella, the beloved rather than the male lover. Her birthday is coming
up and her uncle, Messala, is taking her to the countryside. The poem
is a reflection of Propertius 2.19, in which Cynthia, Propertius' girl,
was also going to the country. Propertius and Sulpicia discuss the
trip in mirrored ways: Propertius consoles himself with the belief
that boring rurality will hold no temptations for his beloved, whereas
Sulpicia braces herself at the prospect of tedious days and nights spent
at the farm and the cold river of Arretium. Jealousy is the topic of 3.16
and 3.17, thus connecting Sulpicia with both elegiac lover and elegiac
beloved. Both were known to be tormented by insecurity.

Sulpicia's *puella* has a confident and assertive voice which is in
itself unsettling enough. When the *puellae* speak, always through
their poet-lovers, what we get is not, as a rule, flattering for the girls.
Propertius 1.2 sticks out in this respect. He is late, and as he enters,
his eyes fall on Cynthia asleep on the couch. Propertius is transfixed
by her beauty, but frightened at the thought of the abuse he would
receive the moment Cynthia opens her eyes and her mouth (18). Ovid's
heroines in the *Heroides* are also girls with a voice. But for all the
panache of his ingenuous experiment of ventriloquism, the heroines

are often trapped, vainly waiting for an absent companion. Sulpicia is all of them: the elegist, the heroine, the elegists' *puella*; it is the combination of all these roles in one voice that makes Sulpicia so startling. If the male elegists' counter-cultural posture has its dangers, we can imagine the considerable risks that Sulpicia, a respectable daughter of the Roman elite, was undertaking with her unconventional poetry and flouting of convention. Sulpicia's extant corpus is miniscule. But her independent and sophisticated speech opens a precious window to the erudite world of the real women of the circles that produced Latin love elegy.

3

Propertius Unbound:
A Latin Lover at Rome

Though we have very little biographical information on Propertius about which we can be confident, we do know that Sextus Propertius, in common with his fellow elegists, was born to an equestrian family. He was probably born around 50–45 BCE. Propertius also saw his family entangled in the disruption of the civil wars. It is assumed that Propertius' family lost land as part of the confiscations that took place after the Battle of Philippi (when Octavian and Mark Antony confronted and defeated the assassins of Julius Caesar) and a subsequent short civil war in Italy that ended in the siege of Perusia. Propertius was expected to follow a career in the Forum. His poetry attests friendships with politically engaged people such as Cornelius Gallus (see, e.g. 1.5) and Tullus (see 1.6; 1.22), an ambitious young aristocrat. As an emerging and obviously talented member of the landed elite, Propertius was in a similar position to Tibullus. Tibullus was taken under the wing of Messalla and Propertius found a place in the circle of another powerful man of the arts and close associate of Augustus, Maecenas (as we realise from poem 2.1). Propertius was about ten years younger than Tibullus and, as he started to write, he was faced with a more developed Augustan regime. Propertius was still a young adult when Actium (31 BCE) ushered in the Augustan age. Propertius' first book of elegies, the *Monobiblos*, was published probably c. 29 BCE, but his engagement with the new age and its political messages is more apparent in the later books. His reaction contrasts markedly with the dreamy reflection and gentle sadness of Tibullus' poetry. Instead, we get a different, more violent range of emotions.

Propertius is the Latin love elegist par excellence. The exclusive devotion to the girl (*puella*) and the elegiac tropes of the locked out lover (*amator exclusus*), the slavery of love (*servitia amoris*) and the service to love (*militia amoris*) that feature in Tibullus' poetry are with Propertius exquisite, self-referential, formal episodes in which Propertius is a virtuoso. Such literariness is a signature feature of the genre. He is also more clearly in the margins of political life, and from that marginal position (of Rome, but not at its centre; of the elite, but not participating in formal political life), his poems engage in, and perhaps even create, a sense of a counter-culture, a cultural opposition which was to become central to Ovid's elegiac writings. Yet, it makes little sense to limit our readings of Propertius through a political label (say, pro-Augustan/anti-Augustan). His politics (like our politics) is often complex, self-contradictory and confusing. He seems to dare us to pin him down to see through the artifice to a political engagement which is always ultimately poetic. As with Catullus, sex, politics and poetry exist in tension, the creative energies feeding off each other and giving Propertian verse its polished passion.

This chapter traces the Propertian persona. Propertius seems to take us (and himself) on a journey of identification, as we come to know more of his complex personality, of his losses and desires, and the difficulties he has in engaging in an increasingly totalitarian Augustan world. We follow the winding and narrow path of his journey, encountering inversions and regressions. It is a path that fills three Propertian books, but in the fourth book of elegies, Propertius puts the first-person narrative aside, and we lose the poet's voice and identity in a masqued ball, perhaps an acknowledgement that the elegiac persona struggles in this Augustan age. Here, though, we will concentrate on the first three books and begin not with Propertius' paradigmatic opening poem (1.1), in which he announces his hatred of chaste girls, his subservience to love and his devotion to Cynthia, but with the dark ending of the *Monobiblos*, poems 1.21–2, which colour all that has gone on before with a pervasive sense of loss.

The death of love

Poems 1.21 and 1.22 have traditionally been read as a unit, and for a good reason. They refer to the same event, the siege of Perusia in 41–40 BCE, and the death of a particular soldier in the aftermath of this seige, Gallus. The poems are complex and difficult, not least in deciding the person of the narrator, but they provide us with autobiographical information and it is in that deep personal connection to the events that Propertius' voice shines through. The siege of Perusia was the continuation of a long period of traumatic political violence that had shaken Rome since the death of Julius Caesar in March 44 BCE. The period saw three phases of civil war, death squads searching the streets of Rome and scouring the fields of Italy, confiscations of land, displacement of populations and seizures of property. The Perusine war broke out in complex circumstances. Octavian declared his intention to confiscate land to give to veterans, but ended up in conflict with Lucius Antonius, brother of Mark Antony. That conflict escalated into violence, which meant that at one stage as many as six separate armies congregated on central Italy.

The major conflict, however, was between Octavian and Lucius Antonius, and it came to a head at Perusia. Lucius Antonius marched his troops into the hill town of Perusia in the autumn of 41 BCE, perhaps little expecting Octavian and his general Agrippa to besiege the town through the long, cold winter months. By midwinter, with food running out and no hope of relief from sympathetic armies camped to the north, Lucius launched several daring attempts to break the siege. None were successful, and early the following year Lucius surrendered. Octavian forgave Lucius' army and preserved the life of Lucius, but torched the town, sentenced the entire council of Perusia to death and is said to have slaughtered many of Lucius' political allies. Among the many traumas of the period of civil wars, Perusia was marked in Roman consciousness as one of the darker episodes. In 1.22, Propertius embraces not his girl but Perusia, the place and the event, in a poem that not only invokes civil war, death and loss, but forces us to reread and rethink the book we have just read:

> From where and of what quality my family comes,
> Tullus and who are my household gods
> you ask in the name of our never ending friendship.
> If the Perusian graves of our country are known to you,
> Italy's funeral in hard times
> when Rome's discord was driving her citizens to their ruin,
> and the grief of the Etruscan dust for me was greater,
> it was you that allowed my relative's limbs to disperse;
> you allowed his poor bones to lie exposed with no soil on them.
> Neighbouring Umbria, bordering on the plains below,
> a fertile land, a plentiful land, bore me.

There is in this poem a deep emotional association with Perusia, its suffering a suffering for which, in part, his lifelong friend Tullus is responsible. From this poem, we get to reread the preceding poem (1.21), in which it now seems as if Propertius' lost kinsman takes the stage, himself the speaking subject of the poem:

> You who scramble to avoid a shared fate,
> soldier wounded at the Etruscan mounds,
> why at my groan do you roll swollen eyes?
> I am your fellow soldier from the next regiment.
> So may your parents celebrate your safe return;
> and let your sister sense what happened from your tears:
> That Gallus, though he managed to pull away from the midst of
>   Caesar's swords,
> failed to escape unknown hands;
> and of all the dispersed bones she comes across on the Etruscan hills,
> may she know that these are mine.

These two poems conjure up a world of love, grief and anger that claims Propertius amongst its victims. The death of Gallus in 1.21, killed not in fighting for a cause but by bandits on a hillside outside

Perusia, is a tragic waste, a meaningless death caused by the discord
that tore Rome apart and the social dislocation that came with the war
and allowed bandits to lie in wait for the soldiers fleeing the battle.
Gallus, we are led to believe, is the beloved of the poet's own sister and
his death thus becomes the death of love, his body lost on the hillside,
a death mourned but not through the rites and rituals of a funeral.
Propertius' affinity with Perusia is emotional and geographical: in
1.22 we learn that Propertius' birthplace in Umbria touched upon the
lands of Perusia. In those lands, his heart and his ancestors belong,
but these lands are now marked by death. Through that death, love
(*amor*) and friendship (*amicitia*) are thrown into turmoil. Yet, these
two themes are the constant subject-matter of Propertius' *Monobiblos*
(and are topics that are revisited in his Books Two and Three). The
intensity and passion of *Monobiblos* may look like a celebration of love
and friendship, yet the last poems change our reading: the *Monobiblos*
is suddenly filled with anger and sorrow and the fragility of love and
friendship are dramatically exposed. Let us trace each through the
book.

We start with love – the girl. From the beginning, Cynthia's image
carries a certain menace. She opens the collection as a huntress:
'Cynthia first with her eyes trapped me, the wretched one, touched by
no desire before' (1.1.1–2). Propertius is smitten. Cynthia has captured
her helpless victim, and in fact will keep him prisoner throughout Book
One. Eight lines later, Cynthia is Atalanta, the heroic virgin huntress.
Propertius quickly learns to fear his girl and develops tactics to avoid
arousing the ferocity of his beloved. In 1.3, he is late to an appointment.
Entering the house, he finds her lying on the couch asleep. His gaze is
voyeuristic, suggesting his power. He has the urge to give his passive,
defenceless girl a kiss but he pauses: 'And I did not dare to disturb my
lady's rest, fearing her expert ferocity in rows' (1.3.17–18). But even
so, he does not escape. Woken up by the moonlight, Cynthia rests her
elbow on the sofa and snaps at him, totally unimpressed by his adoring
vigil:

At last, harsh retort has pushed you back to our bed,
now that another woman's door is closed in your face!
Where have you wasted the long hours of the night that was mine?
Alas for me, you are now spent as the stars have faded away.

1.3.35–8

Similar warnings are extended to Bassus, a friend and fellow poet,
known for his invective verse. Bassus has been trying to lure Propertius
away from Cynthia with the promise of other girls. Propertius responds
by deploying a principal elegiac *topos*: he is a slave of love, happy to stay
in bondage for the rest of his life. Cynthia is unique; no other girl can
replace her (note the exclusivity of lover/beloved). However, when he
comes to describe it, this singularity is rather ambiguous:

And you will not get away with it.
The girl will find out about your crazed suggestions
and she will prove not a quiet enemy for you.
Cynthia won't trust me with you, and she will not see you, after this.
She will remember such crime.
In her wrath, she'll denounce you to all other girls.
Alas, you will be welcome on no doorstep.

1.4.17–22

In case the message has not been received, Propertius broadcasts the
awesome qualities of his girl in the next poem (1.5) to another friend,
Gallus, possibly the victim of poem 1.21. Gallus seems keen to plunge
into the passions of love and even to court Propertius' girl. Propertius
defends his love and his relationship with a series of images that sound
much more like cautions propelled by bitterly gained wisdom:

Poor man, you rush to be acquainted with the deepest hurt
…
She is not like your other fickle girls, when you meet her;
She does not know how to be soft in anger.
…
There will be no more sleep for you. Your eyes will never be free of her.

By herself, she binds the minds of fierce men.

…

Your strong words lost in a moan,
poor wretch, you won't know who or where you are.

…

And if you give the smallest hint of guilt,
your great name will be embroiled in rumours in no time.

This is a chilly description indeed of a prospective lover, but also describes a current lover. Now we, together with Gallus, can understand Propertius' ominous pallor and skeletal appearance (1.5.21–2). Ill health, inarticulacy, bad reputation and self-doubt erode the lover's identity, plunging him into doubt as to who and where he is. The love that stamped on Propertius' head in 1.1 is gradually destroying him. Cynthia is awesome, attractive and dangerous, dreaded and desired, and always out of control. And yet, Propertius submissively, happily, perseveres. In 1.6, an invitation from Tullus, his politician friend and the addressee implicated in the Perusine massacre in 1.22, for Propertius to accompany him on a trip to the East is turned down. Propertius cannot leave; he is bound in his amatory liaison. As the nephew of the Lucius Tullus who was consul in Asia in 33 BCE, Tullus was the perfect conduit into the political establishment and a political career. Refusing Tullus becomes more significant. Propertius weighs his options: a political career and official recognition and success, a life approved and lived within the conventions of traditional Roman society, or Cynthia. No choice at all. Clearly, our poet is not edging closer to the nascent regime of Octavian-soon-to-be-Augustus or, if he has set his eyes on advancement, he is going about it in a very strange way. In 1.7 he advocates the virtues of love elegy over epic to Ponticus, another poet friend who was composing an epic on the Seven Against Thebes. The advancing of love poetry over the kind of poetry that extolled traditional martial values may have been a taxing read for Maecenas, Propertius' patron (or soon to be patron) and Augustus' good friend.

But Propertius has a very clear idea as to the benefits of love poetry. As he explains to Ponticus:

> I, as is my habit, keep fuelling my passions
> and seek ideas to impress a harsh mistress.
> I am forced to serve my suffering rather than my wit
> and to complain about the hardships of youth.

1.7.5–8

If Propertius/the lover's person and personal reputation are in tatters (at least in traditional eyes), his poetry is not. It is in verse that he can seek ways to control the flighty girl and console himself with illusions of dominance. A few lines later, the project becomes meatier and Propertius allows himself a little grandeur. Propertius fashions himself as the patron of the neglected, suffering lovers who would pore over his manual for advice and comfort: 'May a neglected lover read me regularly, after these, and benefit from recognising my calamities' (1.7.13–14). Failing in love, he prospers in poetry. In this poem on poetry, the fundamental purposes of elegy have been found, as ever subservient to the drama of love; not so much a cure of love as a means of sharing a common problem.

In poem 1.8b this newly-found confidence continues to find voice. From 1.8a, we know already that Cynthia has plans to go abroad with a rich lover. Propertius has the opportunity to develop the *topos* of the poor lover, unable to compete with the gifts of the rich and successful by which his girl is tempted. But the denouement of the crisis is happy. Cynthia is not going abroad after all. She has changed her mind (1.8b.1–2). Why? Well, obviously not because of Propertius' non-existent money or promises of a life of luxury and presents: 'I could not soften her will with gold or Indian pearls but only with flattering verse' (1.8b.39–40). His secret weapon is poetry. And Propertius bursts into a celebratory stanza brimming with self-assurance – and ambiguity:

> So the Muses do exist, and Apollo is not slow to help the lover;
> Supported by them, I love; Cynthia, so rare a woman, is mine.

Now I can touch the highest stars in heaven.
Whether day or night has come, she's mine.
No rival can steal my sure love;
that glory shall meet my oldest age.

　　　　　　　　　　　　　　　　　　　　1.8b.41–6

Perhaps the first expression of unqualified satisfaction in the whole of the book, this utterance stops us in our tracks and makes us re-examine what we have read. And as we do so, the equivocal language emerges: the Muses and the god of poetry, Apollo, have rewarded Propertius. The gift is Cynthia, won by poetry and secured from the entrapments of a life of wealth and status. But the Muses and Apollo provide inspiration and that inspiration allows the girl to be written up, fashioned by the poet-lover as he desires her. Here, then, is a contradiction. The girl who was so stroppy, fiery, and unpredictable in the earlier poems, the harsh lady who captured Propertius, is now herself captured and belongs to him. This is his 'true love': a written girl (a *scripta puella*, 2.10.8), a poetic construct, a book of poems, but it is not the same as the girl that we have encountered in the past few poems. His reputation is made in poetry and in that poetry Cynthia is being remade and recaptured, but the woman who unmakes him, who has power over him and reduces him to the wreck which is poetically inspiring, is somehow lost.

Not surprisingly, then, Cynthia starts fading in the later stages of the book. In 1.15, she is reluctant and slow to rush to his bedside as he lies ill. The poet is gutted by this betrayal (1.15.2). But he is also tormented by suspicions: in the end Cynthia does arrive, but spends more time in front of the mirror than with him. And what is this new pearl necklace that she is wearing? Perhaps a present from a new lover (1.15.7–8)? In 1.17, the poet is caught up in a storm at sea. From his distressed words, we are to understand that he is fleeing Cynthia: 'Since I was able to flee my girl, I deserve to be calling out now to forsaken sea birds' (1.17.1–2). For the rest of the poem, Propertius is trying to lull himself with fantasies of Cynthia's devotion to his memory, but the stark reality cannot be escaped: he is alone in the sea, rejected by, and rejecting,

the artificiality of the female voice
+ **

Cynthia, and the poem immediately following does nothing to mitigate this loneliness; rather the opposite. In fact, now the poet seeks solitude. The girl he had captured seems somewhat less captured now. The chaste devotion of the imagined, written Cynthia has evaporated, and the readers, lapping up their shared woes, have disappeared. Instead, Propertius has a life in the margins, on cold cliffs and rough paths, in the quiet of solitude where his timid voice can at last be heard by the birds nesting nearby (1.18.25–30). Thus withdrawn, he can indulge again in his love, which – the same as in 1.8b that we saw above – is not the contemptuous and fickle Cynthia; it is rather a figment of the poet's imagination and of his art, a *Cynthia* sculpted on the bark of the luscious trees that surround his lonely abode in the woods.

> Ah, how often in your tender shade [beeches and pines] my words
>   reverberate.
> And written in your tender bark is *Cynthia*.
>
> 1.18.21–2

Cynthia, the fearsome, tempestuous girl, is replaced with the *Cynthia* engraved on the tree trunks and the echo of her name bouncing on the rocks. The Cynthia of the city has become a *Cynthia* of woods and pastoral. As Propertius puts it, addressing his unruly beloved:

> Yet, be whatever you may, may the woods resonate for me *Cynthia*
> And may the wild, deserted rocks never be free of your name.
>
> 1.18.31–2

The pastoral framework of the rustic Propertius recalls Virgil and the *Eclogues*. In Chapter 2, we saw Tibullus flirting with the world of the *Eclogues* and with the art represented by them. This was a Callimachean world of sensitivity, but Tibullus' passion for Delia chased him out of Arcadia's serenity and contentment. Their elegiac predecessor, Gallus, found that his passion for Lycoris drove him from Arcadia in *Eclogue* 10. Now, we find Propertius finding his way into the Callimachean Arcadia, and carving Cynthia's name on trees. He can only live away from the city if he has a *scripta puella*. The real girl is decidedly missing. For all his proclamations that he can write the girl, the girl herself appears unwilling to oblige. As Propertius enters the restful shrine of Callimachean sensitivity and Roman new poetry, the spectre of Cynthia is lurking behind *Cynthia*. But behind Cynthia, after the toils and travails of love, there lurks yet darker spectres: the ghosts of Perusia and the dead Gallus call out to Propertius. He reminds his friend Tullus of the loss and the bones on the hillside that cannot properly be mourned. The shady boughs of the poet's repose start to look like an escape from a horror which always threatens to drag him back.

The Roman Callimachus

Although the *Monobiblos* shows variety and some inconsistencies in narrative shape (mainly that not all poems are about Cynthia, and other topics are revisited repeatedly), critics have tended to read the book as a continuous ode – mixing praise with despair – to Propertius' great and only love, Cynthia. Some of the older schools of thought have even suggested that Cynthia is the poetic pseudonym of an identifiable Roman woman by the name of Hostia. In spite of the literary conventions and the identification of Cynthia as a *scripta puella* (as we explored above), Propertius' *Monobiblos* does read at times as a colourful confessional, with a realism grounding the more literary concerns. Yet, even for its flashes of realism, it is hardly a realistic account of a love affair. It is difficult, for instance, to imagine that Propertius carved Cynthia's name into the bark of trees in his lovelorn retreat. The neoteric affiliations and political complexities of the elegists open more flexible and interesting readings of this bohemian, intense love poetry: does it ultimately matter whether there was a 'real' Cynthia? What we have is the poetry and the poetry makes Cynthia for us. What is more important for us, nowadays, is what these poet-lovers say (or, indeed, do not say) with their love poetry rather than any biographical elements buried in the texts.

With Book Two comes a change of tone. Any veneer of realism slips away and Cynthia is a more fleeting presence. The concerns of 2.1 are clear and they have nothing to do with Cynthia:

> You ask me where I get the inspiration to write so often about love
> and how this soft spoken book emerges from my mouth.
> Neither Apollo nor Calliope sing these words to me;
> the girl itself instils in me my wit.
>
> 2.1.1–4

A girl is mentioned, but not named. Wherever she goes, however she acts, whatever she says, the poet is fired up – but not with love for her, rather with passion for verse: 'whatever she does or whatever she says, a great story is born from nothing' (2.1.15–16). The girl is the Muse; she replaces Apollo and Calliope, the conventional (authoritative) sources of inspiration, because the poetry of Propertius is not conventional poetry sanctioned by the gods of poetry. A bold description of Propertius' poetic ambitions emerges halfway through the poem:

> But neither could Callimachus with his narrow breast thunder
> those Phlegrean thunders of Jove and Enceladus
> nor do I have the strength to trace back Caesar's line
> in hard verse to Phrygian ancestors.
> The sailor talks of strong winds, the farmer of his oxen;
> the soldier counts wounds, the shepherd counts sheep;
> but we turn over battles in a narrow bed.
> Let everyone spend the day with whatever art we can.
>
> 2.1.39–46

The above lines are programmatic. Propertius follows the narrow paths of Callimachus, the patron saint of Alexandrianism, avoiding the crass loudness of hackneyed themes and safe, dull repetitions, such as the *Gigantomachy* alluded to in line 39. Propertius' provocation does not even spare the sacred foundational myths of Rome: he cannot raise the strength to trace Caesar's Julian genus back to his famous ancestor, Aeneas (through the latter's second son Iulus). Of course, such a story does exist for us in the text of Virgil's *Aeneid*, and Virgil's national epic (published posthumously in 19 BCE) may already have been the talk of the poetic town. The juxtaposition of Virgil's endeavour and Propertius' retreat loads Propertius' text with political meaning. Propertius signals his refusal (*recusatio*), a fundamental poetic gesture that had already been sanctioned as 'revolutionary' in the Prologue of the Hellenistic poet Callimachus' *Explanations* (*Aetia*).

But if in the third-century BCE world of Callimachus and his fellow aesthete poets this resistance was primarily aesthetic, in Rome of the 30s and 20s BCE epic poetry was an important contribution to the political atmosphere fostered by the Augustan regime. Thus *recusatio* was a political gesture, saying 'no' to a powerful political regime and thereby asserting Propertius' independence and offering a challenge to the regime's power. Not everything was to be decided on the battle-field; some problems were solved in bed. The *recusatio* exists in an in-between zone of politics and literature. Virgil's *Eclogue* 6 from c. 40 BCE, perhaps the most quoted Roman neoteric *recusatio*, had furnished the neoteric textbook with an elegant example of the political-in-the-artistic which would have still been fresh in the readers' memories. Propertius generates a distance in his *recusatio* and in the space that he opens up, there is the possibility of some freedom, and of finding a distinctive poetic voice. Yet, such freedoms would appear to come at the cost of discomfiting the masters of Rome.

But we are never too far from a twist, an unexpected tour de force, with Propertius. A little further though the scroll of Book Two comes a rather perplexing poem, 2.10. After all the passionate declarations of Callimachean devotion with which he started the book, here Propertius seems to go back on his word as he declares readiness for national, patriotic composition.

> But it is time to dance round Helikon with other metres;
> now is the moment to give the field to the Haemonian horse.
> Now it pleases me to mention troops strong in battle
> and speak of my leader's Roman expeditions.
> But if my strength is found wanting my courage is surely laudable,

the mere intention to sing of great themes is enough.
Let first youth sing of Love, and old age sing of commotion.
I will sing of wars now that my girl is written up.

2.10.1–10

What a reversal, we marvel! Renowned for their strength, the
Haemonian horses point to epic poetry. Grandiose verse by Propertius
will at last be heard on Helicon, the mountain of the nine Muses. But
where has the bravado of the poet whose vocation has been to enjoy
love gone? And what about the promises for humble, subtle poetry in
the narrow streets of the Callimachean community? And, most impor-
tantly, where has Cynthia gone? In her place we have a *scripta puella*, a
written woman, whose script is now concluded. But Propertius' intent
is already inflected by fears of his weakness: what if he just cannot write
the epic? He will at least be praised for his intentions, will he not? Yet,
ten lines later, he is giving up hope:

As, when the head of a great statue cannot be reached,
a wreath is placed before its lowly feet,
so we today, unable to mount the song of praise,
give cheap incense, from a poor man's offering.
For my songs are not yet acquainted with Ascra's fountain;
love has only washed them in Permessus' stream.

2.10.21–6

The poem that started with a yearning for panegyric finishes with a
declaration of the poet's deficiency. Songs dipped in the water of Ascra
(Hesiod's hometown in Boiotia, mainland Greece) are here meant to be
understood as songs constructed in the grave Hesiodic style. But the
poet has not yet drunk from the sources of Hesiod. His poems have
only been dipped in the stream of Permessus, where, as Virgil tells us,
Gallus, the early elegist, once wandered. The complexity of the expla-
nation baffles us: praise is cheap, if not done to the highest standard
(one wonders how much of Horace and Virgil Propertius would
find 'cheap'). Love poetry is only a poor substitute, and yet, one that

Propertius will continue to write. 'No change there then,' Maecenas, Propertius' patron, might have been tempted to mumble. But perhaps Maecenas should have been thankful. This second *recusatio* (for it is a form of *recusatio*) points us back to the first (2.1) and specifically lines 17–36, which come before the refusal to write epic poetry. In the course of a carefully constructed aside to Maecenas, Propertius does offer his poetic services to Augustus and the regime.

> But even if the Fates, Maecenas, had given me the power
> to lead heroic forces to war,
> I would not sing of Titans and Ossa on Olympus,
> for Pelion to be a road to heaven
> or ancient Thebes or Pergama that gave Homer fame,
> or two seas joining at Xerxes' order,
> or Remus' first kingdom or the pride of lofty Carthage,
> the menace of Cimbri, the German tribe, and Marius' good deeds:
> No, I would commemorate your Caesar's wars and deeds, and you
> would be my second concern, under all-mighty Caesar.
>
> 2.1.17–26

Praise at last, it seems. But this is a poem set in a negative key, refusing to write epic and listing the epics that he would not write, an aggressive, assertive negativity that distances Propertius from the values of the regime. He would not write epic, neither mythical (the references are to *Theogony*'s Titans, or *Iliad*'s Pergama) nor historic (Remus stands out here and, of course, lofty Carthage). And yet, he would write and praise Caesar (Augustus) and Maecenas, his right hand, but not in the traditional form that such praise has tended to be packaged: mythical/ historical epics of national identity. It seems that even when he co-opts his poetry to the emerging regime, Propertius still does it 'his way'. Reading on, he provides us with some clues for the Propertian epic:

> For anytime I sang of Mutina or Philippi, where the bodies of Rome
> are buried,
> or of the naval battles with Sicilian refugees
> and of the overturned hearths of the ancient Etruscan race

and the captured shores of Ptolemaic Pharos
or of Egypt and the Nile, when he was dragged into the city,
flowing along powerless, with seven channels captive,
or of the necks of kings encircled with gold chains
and of Actian prows sailing the Sacred Way,
my Muse would always weave you into these wars.

                                                              2.1.27–35

Propertius shows no reticence, no holding back. We get details of
Augustus' involvement in vicious civil wars of national disunity – of
Romans killing Romans at Mutina and Philippi and the seas of Sicily
(the latter a slave war in Augustan versions of history) and also the
disastrous war of Perusia (where old Etruscan hearths were turned
over to burn the city) and the war of Actium – before an account of the
lavish triumph of 28 BCE for victories in Egypt. This eulogy is a mixed
blessing. Bitter reminders of Octavian's rise are paraded before us, with
the violence of the civil wars overshadowing the processions for victory
in Egypt. It is hardly a song of national unity.

A new poetic-political form emerges in this poem. Propertius
will explicitly *not* glorify the Roman past. He will *not* replicate the
historical epics that flourished in the Republican years with writers
such as Ennius and Naevius. He will *not* find great mythic cycles to
retell. He will *not* engage with the foundational myths of Rome. So in
this stream of rejection, what will be the new epic form? We can look
forward to 2.10 and Propertius' failed decision to sing about Caesar.
Augustan epic cannot be written. The confusing diversity of the rest
of Book Two can now be read in a different light. Propertius gradually
distances himself from Cynthia, the woman and the verse, flirting
instead with the establishment. But in 2.31, he is late again for one of
their rendezvous (as in 1.3). His excuse is that he was at the opening
of the portico of Apollo's temple. The temple was closely connected to
Octavian's own house and was constructed as something of a victory
monument to the god with whom Octavian most closely associated
himself in the years from 44 to 31 BCE and whom he credited with

the Actian victory. The demands of the Forum appear to be winning over desire for the girl. Propertius has no compunctions to explain to Cynthia why he was detained; a far cry from his reticent, timid vigil of 1.3. And yet, he tells us in 2.12, Love never abandons him. 'Alas, he never flies off from my breast' (2.12.15).

Cynthia continues to move through Propertius' verse till the end of the book, but more often than not, even when she is present, he talks about poetry, the art of writing about love, and even other girls; the characteristic exclusivity of the affair is fading. He starts Book Three by invoking his Hellenistic forefathers, the scholar-poets of Alexandria:

> Ghosts of Callimachus and sacred rites of Coan Philetas
> I pray that you let me enter into your grove.
> I step in, first, as priest of a pure fountain
> to present Italian mysteries with Greek dances.

3.1.1–4

Once again, we are prompted to believe that the lines have been drawn neatly. Propertius will now be the Roman Callimachus, transposing pure (Alexandrian) poetry to Rome. Even so, the play with convention and innovation, civic concerns and private indulgence continues. After the programmatic poems 1, 2 and 3, in which Propertius asserts his belief in, and knowledge of, the minutiae of Alexandrian art (its symbols, mythic landscapes, images, metaphors, the lot), we read an array of poems on a variety of topics. We get a careful relay of Caesar's plans for war with India (3.4), immediately preceding an ode to peace which he (the poet) and his fellow lovers worship (3.5). Further along, we get an elaborate description of a rather undignified brawl he had with his girl on a street corner (3.8), thus bringing to the fore the map of a chaotic and anarchic lovers' Rome that Augustus was keen on eradicating. After this idle, naughty moment comes praise of Maecenas, wrapped inside another *recusatio* which trusts that his long-suffering patron will understand if Propertius feels the need to be 'occupied on a little [Alexandrian] river' (3.9.36). Of course Propertius would obey

(3.9.46–57), but Maecenas's considerate attitude to youth was such that he could not act the tyrant and insist: 'Patron of early youth, use soft reins and give me a sign with your right hand when my wheels are let loose' (3.9.52–3). Propertian *recusatio* dares the latent tyranny of the regime which has to adhere to its proclaimed non-tyranny by allowing Propertius his Callimachean style. The circularity is perfect, and a chase of political loyalty, poetic form, freedom and Propertian distance dominates the book.

*   *   *

When reading poetry, it is tempting to try and fix the poet's position in relation to ideas and ideology. The temptation is to read the poems as biography. But the absence of that fixity in Propertius frustrates our desire for a straightforward interpretation that would allow us to say that, at last, we understand the poet. This frustration creates a further temptation to read his work as playful, thus disrupting our desire to know the man behind the first-person voice of the poet. A poet who refuses to commit, politically and personally, whose flag cannot be nailed to any mast, seems not to be a serious man. In place of commitment, we find irony, and irony is associated too often in our modern world with a lack of meaning and with an all too easy political and social quiescence. Yet, Propertius' 'games' are far from straightforward manifestations of a (neoteric) propensity to ironic (perhaps subversive) wit. Instead, we can read the lack of fixity in Propertius' multiple voices and subject-positions as a struggle with an *aporia*, an indecision. That indecision reflects his position in an uncertain and fragmented environment. After all, what kind of epic could he write in the post-revolutionary period? Did the old stories have any meaning in the Augustan world? Would an epic soaked in the blood of the civil wars and polluted by the overturned hearths of Perusia not be an epic of Roman destruction (a multiplied, replayed account of the fall of Rome), and how would such a poem sit in the new Augustan world?

The Roman revolution changed the rules of Roman society and threw into question the relationship of an individual and the city of Rome itself. This was not a matter of constitutional change, but of politics and the individual. The Augustan revolution offered an image of what it was to be a Roman, the duties of a Roman man, and a reading of the history of the city that formed collective memory. But all these narratives of identity were in the process of creation in the Augustan city. Augustan monuments, coins, statues, political pronouncements, legislation and political acts were establishing a version of the city before the eyes of Augustus' contemporaries. In Books Two and Three we see Propertius exploring his place within that world. In 2.7, for example, he rejoices at the failure of Augustan legislation in marriage (probably c. 28 BCE). Augustus would get his way a decade later. But the law would end Cynthia and Propertius is not prepared to give her up. He comes down the hill from the opening of Apollo's temple to Cynthia's bed, late perhaps, but still there. We can read Propertius as *scriptus poeta*, the written poet, a character in search of a narrative. It is not that there is an absence of narratives: the *recusatio* lists so many possibilities. But none of those narratives fit. The Augustan narrative lay all around, increasingly dominant in the Roman landscape, increasingly felt through Roman law, increasingly pressurising the artist. The uncertainty of the poetic persona reflects a narrative world-in-creation in which meanings, traditions and truths have only a spurious certainty. The flexible, uncertain and undecided Propertius is a man lost in his times, and in his dislocation we find a sensitive and serious elegiac voice.

4

Love-games and Power-games:
Ovid and the Politics of Desire

The brief and intense life-cycle of Latin love elegy comes to a sparkling end with Ovid – and what a denouement! With Ovid, the rules of the game, never settled in this wayward genre, are blown apart and rewritten in the service of an author who is every bit as dark and uncomfortable as he is witty and irreverent. First things first, and a few words on the life of the *enfant terrible* of Latin literature. Born in 43 BCE, at Sulmo, east of Rome, in the shadow of the site of Julius Caesar's assassination, Ovid was still just a child by the time Octavian cemented his grip on power, only 12 years old when Octavian defeated Mark Antony and his Egyptian queen at the naval Battle of Actium.

In many ways he is very similar to the other elegists: born into a wealthy equestrian family and destined for the legal profession by his father, he instead was attracted by the literary bohemia of his time. He had friends in both Messala's and Maecenas' circles; Propertius and Horace, amongst others, are mentioned in his poetry as like-minded spirits (see, for example, his autobiographical poem *Tristia* 4.10.41–54). A bit like Catullus, Ovid frustrated familial and social expectations, choosing the life of writing and artistic endeavour over the Forum. In fact, the Roman Forum will be subjected to irreverence in Ovid's love poetry, emerging as an implausibly conducive environment for matters of the heart, rather as a space in which the young, upcoming citizen showcases his expensive education and literary and other talents in unorthodox ways. But the heartache and anger of Catullus' poetry has been dissipated, as has Tibullus' melancholy *aporia* in the new, puzzling world; nor do we have Propertius' bitter explosions and hard-faced irony at the constraining of the Roman lover. There is an able treatment of emotion in Ovid's elegiac poetry, both mesmerising and intriguing. Irony instils lightness to his work of love; but alongside this gossamer touch come darker shades in a love affair vulnerable to violence and drawn into games of power.

*   *   *

We who were once Ovid's five slender volumes
Are now three: that's how the author preferred us to be.
So, even if there is still no pleasure for you in the reading of us,
yet, the punishment will be lighter with two books less.

This playful prefix to the first book of a three-book collection of 'Loves' (*Amores*) alerts the reader of its author's self-deprecation. We are told that our text is a compression from five to three books and thus already a partial narrative, with elements removed from our view, though we cannot guess as to the editorial rationale. We do not know much about the earlier incarnation of the 'Loves' but it was probably published gradually in the course of the teens of the first century BCE. The second edition, the one we have, is believed to have been published just a few years before the end of the first century. The beloved is called Corinna, only she comes into the collection very 'late', in poem 1.5, and not announced, perhaps even proclaimed, from the very first lines, as we saw with Propertius and his Cynthia. She also leaves too 'early' and that should give us some reason for concern. The third book is essentially not about her, but what is it about? Is elegy not the frustrated yearnings for a happy life with the beloved anymore?

First things first: the editing process invites us to read the poems against each other, as comprising a carefully constructed narrative: poems 1–5 of *Amores* 1 are clearly a group. Poem 1 puts the reader on her guard:

I was getting ready to produce in solemn verse a story of arms
and violent war with a metre matching the subject matter,

the second verse equal to the first; Cupid laughed
(they say) and stole one foot away.

1.1.1–4

What is missing here is as important as what is actually there. Arms and war and violence were going to be the subject matter of the new collection, a clear allusion to the opening lines of the *Aeneid* ('I sing of arms and man'). The allusion draws attention to what, or rather who, is omitted: there is no man in the programmatic opening line, and nor is there a girl! But when we compare Ovid and Propertius, as surely we are invited to, the absence of the girl (and the boy) contrast with the presence of the third character in Propertius' opening lines, Cupid. Ovid's Cupid is the naughty boy who steals one of the six metrical feet of the hexameter line to give the poem its distinctive elegiac unevenness. The line is shortened and instead of the smooth epic the limping elegiac couplet materialises. Ovid is dragged to write love elegy, kicking and screaming. Curiously, after 20 or so lines of fluent elegy, Ovid realises that he does not actually have the right material for the new genre ('And I have no material that would fit that more slender line', 1.1.19); with material Ovid here means none else than 'a boy, or a girl with beautifully combed, long hair' (1.1.20). We are told that the beloved is in fact desired but only in so far as it might be a fascinating subject for Ovid's artistic endeavours. Ovid needs a lover so as to write love poetry, rather than writing love poetry because of his lover. Whereas Propertius is captured by Cynthia, and turned to elegy, Ovid is captured by poetry and turned to love.

Indeed, the *puella* does arrive by 1.3 but she is still anonymous. She is to be seduced by verse – 'Give yourself to me, a happy subject for my song' (1.3.19) – to produce an early version of celebrity seduction (sleep with me and I'll make you famous). A litany of declarations of devotion, loyalty, monogamy (1.3.11–18) culminates with a typically Ovidian twist that deflates the passion and jeopardises the sincerity of any statement. Can we trust anything this poet-lover tells us? Love is secondary to literature and a contrivance for literature. Are we watching an invention of love? Or is it a matter of patience: these are still early days, and momentum and honesty and passion might emerge as the love affair gathers power and we move through the collection: after all, we know that there are enough twists and turns for three or five books.

This literary love makes us conscious and suspicious of what is to come, but also encourages us to cast a glance backwards to the preceding poem, 1.2, which opens with (at least the semblance of) heart-felt emotion:

> How can I phrase what is it like, that the mattress seems to me
> so hard, the blankets do not stay in bed, and I spent the night,
> (so long a night) sleepless, and my tired bones hurt
> from the continuous tossing.
>
>   1.2.1–4

Ovid, like other lovers, is rendered an insomniac. But guess what: the angst is short-lived and our belief in its sincerity takes another knock as Ovid hastens to provide his own answer to the (literary) question: 'That's what it is: his slender dart is stuck in my heart. Fierce love tosses my tamed breast' (1.2.7–8). But if we expected a performance of the wounded, enslaved lover raging against this entrapment, we would be disappointed. Unbothered by this psychological revelation, Ovid ponders what to do next, and after only the briefest of hesitations he settles with a solution that shows how different he is determined to be from his love-stricken predecessors:

> Should I give in, or do I, by resisting it, intensify the sudden fire?
> Let's give in: a load endured willingly, is a light load.
> I have seen the flames tossed about by torches swung around grow tall
> and those ones not shaken, I have seen them die.
>
>   1.2.9–12

Metaphors jovially elaborating on the advantages of submission are offered: oxen resisting the yoke suffer much more than those who choose to bear it with a pleasant demeanour (13–14), and a proud horse feels the bridle harder than a submissive one (15–16). Gracefulness and playfulness set the tone for these images, which seem preoccupied with art far more than they are with emotions. Within an atmosphere of a delightful acceptance of the lover's slavery, the main imagery of the poem emerges. Ovid has no need to put up a fight with Cupid and is happy to be part of a triumph for the victorious boy. A Roman metaphor dominates the rest of the poem. Cupid, the triumphant *imperator* (general/emperor) of love, will parade amidst cheering crowds with 'fine troops', Flattery, Error and Fury (35), on his side. But this is a desired defeat and the late-coming inspiration that will allow Ovid to achieve his destiny. The poem indulges in images of a satisfied Cupid, but it is not the kind of imperial representation that would satisfy Augustus too. One is bound to wonder about the reliability of the Roman troops flanking the general – flattery, error and fury – and how Roman readers would have understood such a visual image against their memory of Augustus riding in triumph through the streets of the city. And there is also an air of mental abstraction and self-possession about the victorious boy that, I imagine, would leave Augustus wondering whether to be pleased or annoyed. On the edge of these festivities for a valiant conquest, Ovid remarks: 'No praise for you – unarmed I will be defeated by arms' (1.2.22). The defeated did not fight; and what price a victory over those unwilling to play the game and resist? In the face of the inevitability of defeat, the sensible course is to tow the line and willingly give oneself, but in that willing acquiescence in the triumph of the Cupid Emperor Triumphator there is a sense that the poet is not crushed and that resistance remains. In this peculiar Roman triumph the conquered have willingly offered their hands to the chains, but they have done so to preserve a semblance of freedom.

Amores 1.4 provides ample explanation as to why Ovid might rejoice in the role of the lover-slave. The poem opens with anger, as any reader who had read Propertius would expect. The *puella* has a man (*vir*) – a significant other likely to be her husband – and Ovid torments himself with mental images of the two lovers together (1–10). But as always with Ovid, the 'and yet' is never far off. Self-pity does not suit this lover; by line 11, Ovid springs into action, delivering precise and confident instruction to the girl:

> Still, you must understand what it is to be done by you,
> and do not give my words out to the East or the tepid South wind.
> Arrive before your man. Not that I can see what can be achieved
> by you arriving first. But still arrive before him.
> When his body presses on the couch and you join him with modest face,
> as you take your place on the table, secretly touch my foot,
> watch me, and my nods, and my loquacious face;
> catch my secret messages and send replies.
> …
> Touch the table with your hands, like those who pray
> when you wish many well deserved evils on your husband.
> Whatever he mixes for you, be alert, tell him you'd like him to drink it;
> Lightly ask for what you want from the boy there.
>
> 1.4.11–18, 27–30

If the list of instructions is long (and I have left some out of my extract above), the list of what she should not do is equally exhaustive:

> If by chance he offers you something that he has tried before
> refuse the donated food previously tasted by his lips.
> Don't let him press his arms around your neck
> and do not place your gentle head upon his hard chest.
> Don't let your breasts and your fondlable nipples admit his fingers,
> and – above all – refuse to give a single kiss!
> …
> Do not squeeze thigh to thigh, or mingle legs,
> or link his hard foot with your tender one.
>
> 1.4.33–8, 43–4

Burning with supposed jealousy, Ovid tries to pre-empt and prevent the games of love between *puella* and *vir*, that he knows only too

well ('I am wretched: I fear much because I have done much without
shame', 45). But inadequacy fuels obsessive observation. Being a
nobody in the scene (almost invisible as the lovers play, or refuse to
play, in a seemingly public prelude to sex), Ovid enjoys a paradoxical
omnipresence, unnoticed, but seeing everything, feeling everything,
from the brush of a hand on the nipples, the touch of thighs and the
hard and soft feet of the man and his girl. In a poem that was a lament
for the lover's impotence, almost every line exudes power and control,
because he can see and instruct and feel. As the poem-lament finishes,
we have ample sense of what the *vir* and the *puella* should be doing
but almost no sense of what the lover actually feels about the girl. The
emotional reticence is enhanced with metapoetic references that divert
our attention to matters of art (for example, with lines that juxtapose
the softness of elegy with the hardness of epic such as l.36: 'do not rest
your gentle head on his hard chest'; or l.44: 'do not link his hard foot
with your tender'). Ovid turns his poem into a choreography of sex,
almost a technical treatise in which the emotional engagement of the
creator, choreographer, observer, is not that of a lover.

In 1.5, the girl breaks cover and is named.

> The heat was bubbling and the mid-time of the day had just passed
> as I was lying in the midst of the bed, to give my limbs a rest.
> One shutter was open, and the other closed;
> like the light in the woods,
> like the twilight that glimmers as Phoebus rushes away,
> or when the night has gone and the day has not yet risen.
> …
> See, in comes Corinna, covered in her loose gown,
> her scattered hair hiding her ivory neck.
> …
> I ripped off her dress; it did not do much harm to its thin texture
> yet by that garment she struggled to be covered.
> And yet she struggled as someone who did not wish to win,
> and she was defeated, not unwillingly, by her self-betrayal.
> When she stood before my eyes, the cloth put aside,

I could not detect a single blemish anywhere on her body.
What shoulders and what arms did I see and touch!
The shape of her nipples seemed made to be pressed!
How flat a belly so smooth under beautifully formed breasts!
What well sculpted flanks! What a fine youthful thigh!
Why enumerate any further details? I did not see anything not worthy
    of praise;
and naked as she was, I pressed her body to my body.
And the rest – who does not know? Exhausted we both rested.

1.5.1–6, 9–10, 13–25

At first sight, the poem shines with uncomplicated delight. The girl is present, consenting, radiant; the poet-lover is smitten; one is left wondering whether this piece of superlative contentment is, in fact, a breach of the rules of love elegy with its flouting of unrequited love. On a second reading we are able to start with the by now familiar 'and yet' clause: 1.5 is so tempting as the locus of fulfilment, the positive counterpart to the frustrated love of 1.4, and yet, a careful rereading punctures the simplicity and questions the realism, and reality, of this seemingly down-to-earth erotic encounter. Midday, mid-summer, half-open windows, light in-between day and night; the liminality of the scene undermines its palpability; we are tempted to read it more as an interstitial epiphany that would refer the knowledgeable reader of the period back to another famous literary tryst, Lesbia's apparition as a goddess with creaking sandals on Catullus' doorstep (68b.70), another scene where fantasy merges with reality to a mesmerising effect.

Later on in his poetry, Ovid will meet another delectable young woman in a skimpy, transparent dress walking in the woods, only that girl is not your everyday girl: Elegy herself will make an apparition in *Amores* 3.1 to tease the poet and lure him into continuing service. Certainty, once more, is withdrawn. Is the girl standing at the threshold of the poet's abode in 1.5 a real girl? The sleepy poet imagines the girl arriving in his bedroom wearing very little: how does she get there? Is she not an erotic daydream? You'd think having a name makes her real, at last. But Corinna is also a derivative from *kore*: 'girl' but also the 'pupil of the eye' in Greek. Is the ethereal apparition then merely a reflection of the poet's own imagination? Poetry about love once again blends into love for poetry, for beautiful art, for impeccable statues. In the sequence of 1.1–4, Ovid has tried our patience, preparing us to meet the girl, only for us to be met with poetic materials instead. In 1.5 we get a detailed description of impeccable body: arms, shoulders, belly, breasts and waist – but no face, no mouth that could utter words of love in reciprocation. We see in her inhuman perfection, laid before our eyes in a way that makes us, the readers, voyeurs in this pornography (writing of the woman), but a woman whose passivity in her nudity recalls statues not lovers. Is it possible that even in this, most sensual of encounters so far, we are still in the realm of artistic creation?

If we are meant to read Corinna as a real girl, we might infer her reality from the single dark moment of the poem, ll.13–16: the poet snatches the gown and pulls it off, doing it only little harm. The girl resists and tries to cover herself again but then yields and stands naked in front of the poet. The poet clearly wants to believe, and show, that the girl was willing, or at least tamed in the process. But is that so, or is this merely a projection convenient for the poet-lover? In a poem where we never hear the girl speak, we will never know. The violence of love makes here a momentary, disturbing, apparition, reminding us of the disconcerting opening lines of *Amores* 1.1: force and violence might indeed be the subject matter of the new collection, even after playful Cupid stole one foot, forcing Ovid away from the king's great deeds and battles. And the hint of violence we detected in 1.5 becomes the subject matter of 1.7. The piece opens with abject remorse from the poet's part:

> Put handcuffs on my hands (they deserve the chains)
> until my fury dissipates, if you, in front of me, are a friend.
> My frenzy moved thoughtless hands against my mistress,
> my girl now weeps, hurt by my mad hands;
> then, I could have either hurt my dear parents;
> or hurled insanely blows at the sacred gods.

> 1.7.1–6

Racked by guilt, the only excuse Ovid can offer is something approximating madness; he was possessed, not himself, when he hit his beloved, like Ajax when he slayed the sheep, mad with grief for losing Achilles' arms (7–8). And was not Orestes prey to the Furies when he prepared that bow with which he killed his mother (9–10)? Coming from the remote world of myth, these pictures are meant to offer something by way of an explanation for the cruel act, but they only add confusion: isn't it a strange tactic to respond to the acute angst and guilt of the moment by flying into the world of myth? And more so, as it is there where the poet finds yet more distractions: Atalanta hunting on the Arcadian mountains, Ariadne weeping for the departing Theseus, the priestess Cassandra (13–18), all pretty reminders of the beauty of the stricken girlfriend, attracting the poet's attention and encouraging a voyeuristic approach to a woman's grief.

The poet's grief becomes both suspect as well as spurious. There is something uncomfortable in his adoration of the frightened maid's face 'all white if it was not for her scratched cheeks' (40). We begin to suspect that sensuality is emerging, that the poet's emotion is now all spent in some perverse pleasure at the aesthetic value of the distraught woman when we get the admission in the poet's approving description of the girl as 'standing all pale ... like a rock taken from a Parian ridge' (51–2) with 'tears flowing down her cheeks like water that flows out of melting snow' (57–8). A poem supposedly about a penitent man atoning for the violence he has inflicted on his girlfriend, transmutes into praise for the girl's beauty-in-anguish: the absorption of grief into a kind of artistic redemption is disconcerting.

Disconcerting is indeed an apt word for the rest of our deliberations with the *Amores* in this chapter. 'Lovers are soldiers' we are told in 1.9.1, and though we recognise this as one of Roman elegy's favourite sayings, what we get in the rest of Book One, and increasingly in Books Two and Three, is a systematic analysis of what becomes of love if we decide to take this playful gesture of blending the erotic with the martial at face value. Persistence, misery, oppression and above all insidious violence are features shared by lovers and soldiers. We are told in the elaborately worked out imagery of 1.9 that 'it is often useful to attack a sleeping enemy and strike unarmed troops with armed hand' (1.9.21–2). Love-as-war is ugly: rape, or something very like it. On its own, the violence is unsettling and demeaning for the men and women involved, as we will see, and so different from the consensual negotiations and games of love that were conducted by the earlier elegists. In this blending of the erotic and the martial, love mirrors politics, and the lovers' erotic misdemeanours stand as a metaphor of a yet more sinister transgression, that of the Roman desire for domination. And this latter message makes it even harder for any reader – least of all Augustus – to dismiss Ovid's *Amores* as frivolous talk in the margins of the respectable Roman way.

Amores 2.13 and 14 are the perfect pair of poems with which to explore this warfare in Ovid's love poetry. In 2.13, Corinna lies exhausted, her life in danger after procuring an abortion (2.13.1–2). Ovid is upset but, as we will see, about pretty much anything else other than her well-being. Corinna has made a risky decision, but Ovid's rage comes from not having been consulted (2.13.3–4). His rights as the father (2.13.5) have been ignored. Indeed, Corinna fades into the background, obscured by Ovid's exhibitionist display of Egyptian lore (13.7–14). His prayers are about her and him in equal measure (15–16). Little by little, the woman in the sick-bed is eclipsed by the lover's male ego. I do not think we can preclude the effect of such tactics. What do these bullish, persistent attempts at keeping the focus on the poet convey: an inflated sense of self-worth, or insecurity fuelled by the lack of control that the poet is faced with? Corinna cut her lover out of her decision. This is a battle of wills and the outcome is not fixed, but it is a battle being fought over Corinna's body.

Poem 2.14 is a rhetorical attempt to prove Corinna wrong for going through with the abortion, but the sick girl has been totally occluded behind the bulk of a moralising and political discourse that uses the issue of abortion for point scoring. The precariousness of power is exposed in this poem. To start with, Corinna, and not the poet, is now the soldier engaged in tactical warfare and she turns the tables on Ovid.

Faced with this reversal, the lover expresses shock, but soon it becomes clear that the shock is not over the loss or even the betrayal, but over the collapse of a sovereign (and absolute) social and political morality. If, for example, abortion was the favourite solution in the olden days, the race of men could well have been eliminated (2.14.9–10); if Venus had made the decision to abort Aeneas, no Caesars would have graced Rome with their presence (2.14.17–18); the girl herself would have died if her mother followed the same tactics (2.14.19–20) and so would the lover himself (2.14.21–2). The conjectures carry on and transpose us to a distant world of mythical creatures (Medea and Procne are enlisted as appropriate parallels) and even the natural world is used as a measure of the extremity of Corinna's gesture (2.14.35–6). Once again the reader's certainties are put to the test: the poet-lover's loud expressions of grief need to be weighed against the exaggerated images that Corinna's abortion has supposedly triggered in the lover's mind. Is the poet-lover truly so upset about what would have happened had Julius Caesar not had the chance to rule Rome? Does that not sound more like the kind of moralising discourse that Augustus would have mobilised against such an affront to his authority? But is Ovid suddenly transformed into Augustus' mouthpiece, or are his elaborate protestations a form of mocking mimicry? Is the prediction of the end of the world latent in this imagery a suitable reaction to Corinna's actions in aborting the illegitimate child of her illegitimate lover, a lover now suddenly transforming himself into a paragon of conservative moral certainties?

In any case, what I do not hear at all is any interest in the girl's own motivations: we are not even sure whose baby that was. Elsewhere Corinna seems married, but here Ovid takes the role of the husband. Context is missing and without context the assertion of power by Corinna, the poet's subject and creation, becomes somehow an act of resistance. Corinna may be written but she is not the poet's and we are drawn to wonder about her life outside the *Amores*: perhaps in those two missing books, and when Corinna resists, the poet becomes Augustus. The male lover is excluded from the female experience.

Amatory warfare maybe a poetic – and political – gesture, but there is clearly a price to be paid in the quality of love. Love wanes in this amorous warfare: after 2.14, Corinna is a fleeting presence, and these rare references relegate her to the past (see, e.g. 2.19.9; 3.1.49; 3.7.25).

Dissatisfaction and distrust permeate Book Three; a couple of examples reveal the disengagement of the lover. In 3.3, the lover suffers the ignominy of being still attracted to someone that has been cheating on him. He is unable to wrench himself away from the beautiful, unfaithful girl, triggering momentary reminders in our mind of Catullus' emotional turmoil at his inability to escape his cheating *puella*. In a desperate gesture towards the end of the poem, Ovid asks the *puella* to hide her infidelity. But in the next poem, 3.4, he elevates what seemed a resigned suggestion to an assertive mechanism of control. By the end of the poem, the cuckolded husband has been advised to either get an ugly wife that will be unable to attract lovers (3.4.41–2), or else embrace his wife's friends and thus improve his social standing in the appropriate circles (3.4.45–8): adultery not marriage is the way to social respectability. The concrete proposals for action are delivered deadpan, in a typical Ovidian fashion, and the reader is, once again, landed with the perplexing task of weeding through the irony to locate the meaning, if, indeed, there is any meaning beyond the irony.

With 3.14, things seem to come to a head. The lover appears distraught, resigned, but – I would say – also humiliated.

> I cannot object to your frolicking: you are beautiful.
> But it is not necessary for me, poor fool, to know.
> My censorship does not demand that you are chaste
> but it does ask that you make at least an attempt to hide it.
> She who can deny that she has erred, has not erred;
> only a fault confessed makes someone notorious.
>
> 3.14.1–6

The tactics are meant to provide peace of mind for the cheated lover through ignorance but, before long, jealousy pops up its ugly head:

Why do I see so many notes received and given?
Why are both sides of the bed messed up?
Why do I have to notice your hair disturbed by more than sleep
and love bites on your neck so clear for all to see?
Only the sin itself you hide from my eyes;
If you do not rush to spare your reputation, please spare me!
I lose my mind and I die every time you confess your wrongdoing.
And through my veins the blood runs cold drop by drop.
Then I love you, and then I hate, in vain what I must love.
Then I wish I were dead but together with you.

3.14.31–40

For all his determination to overlook his beloved's escapades, the poet cannot himself escape the signs of her infidelity. They catch his attention and induce discomfort. The suffering (obviously echoing Catullus 85, 'I love and I hate') does not become the erstwhile 'cool' and blasé poet. In a desperate attempt to free himself from the agony of knowing, he offers himself up to complete and willing manipulation:

I will not inquire about, nor go after, those things that you will be prepared
to hide. To be deceived will feel like a gift to me.
But if you are ever caught in the midst of the sinful act,
and your disgrace is obvious to my eyes,
what I have seen well, deny I have seen well.
My eyes will give in to my words.
The palm is yours to win, if I wish to be beaten.
All you need to remember is the words 'I did not!'

3.14.41–8

There is so much more going on in this poem than merely two lovers' squabbles patched up and made good in the end. As in 1.2, the lover is willingly defeated and led off in triumph, defeated because he has no power to resist and no willingness to fight, but by Book Three, the outrageous proclamation of slavery and the insinuation of servility as the route to freedom have become so much darker. Now, Ovid is paying the prices for his servility, for his losses in the battles of love, and perhaps for the brutalisation of love. The atmosphere of the *Amores* becomes progressively bleaker, and by the time we reach the third book, Corinna and her bodily perfection is only a fond memory as the poet-lover grapples in unsatisfactory encounters with unnamed girls. Poem 3.14 is worthy of special note in its exposure of the staggering failure of the amatory project.

To appreciate this poem fully, we need to go as far back as 2.12. The tone here is important:

> Come, triumphant laurels, crown my temples!
> I have won! Look, Corinna, in my arms,
> whom the husband, the guardian, the stubborn door – so many enemies –
> guarded. No art nor trick of theirs could hold her captive.
> This is a victory worthy of a special triumph,
> in it, whatever else it might be, the spoil is bloodless.
>
> 2.12.1–6

We seem to have a typical Ovidian love poem in which self-confidence, quick wittedness and cunning are enlisted to the pursuit of love. But the poem soon proves to be not about love so much as about a military victory. By far the most powerful emotion on display is glee. The soldier of love has emerged victorious over his many enemies; he is now preparing for the proud parade, a victorious general very much along the lines of Cupid that we encountered at 1.2, who, in his imperial pose, could be seen to be a disconcerting commentary on Augustus. Instead of consummation of his secret and illicit passion, instead of losing himself in awe of his perfect girl, the poet-lover is about to go on parade and assert the social victory of the adulterer. The girl is lost in the power games, turned into yet another form of social corruption.

The death of Elegy

For all their stark differences in tone (2.12 basking in self-assurance, 3.14 wallowing in self-doubt), these two poems are steps along one, inevitable path: that of emotional betrayal and elegiac failure. The path had been laid out by Ovid's elegiac precursors long before Cupid wickedly stole the foot of Ovid's matching couplet and turned the poet to elegy (*Amores* 1.1.1). With the three books of *Amores*, Ovid enriches the elegiac repertory, improvising and improving the stereotypical elegiac formulae and mannerisms; at the same time, though, steadily and often imperceptibly, he works out their extreme conclusion, which is none other than self-destruction. The elegiac plot is tipped over the precipice. The soldiery of love, the slavery to love, the numerous obstacles (the 'madame', the escort, the door, the janitor, to name but a few) all cultivate a plot and poetry that is a kind of crypto-epic, with a climactic end: the girl is denied to the lover, therefore the lover soldier will fight to get the girl. Love is an open competition and there are no rules in this game of conquest.

The more impressive and ingenuous Ovid becomes in his treatment of the amatory mannerisms in the *Amores,* the more discomfort he instils in the elegiac practice of love. *Amores* 3.7 is another such uncomfortable poem of powerlessness, this time expressed through sexual impotence: the lover struggles to cope with his non-perfor-mance ('she was touching me, but not a man was touching her', 43), but he cannot help blaming the *puella* ('Perhaps she did not give up for me her best kisses, she did not pursue me with all her cunning', 55–6). This is an unlikeable liaison that is tainted by distrust and suspicion, and finally explodes in the angry concluding lines:

> 'Why mock me so' she cried, 'or if you're ill,
> who ordered you to place your body, unwillingly, into our bed?
> Either a Circean witch has cast her spells on you
> or you come to me tired from another love.'

> 3.7.77–80

Having barely finished these angry words, the girl (in her 'loose gown' eerily reminiscent of the *puella* of 1.5.9 and her own fluid dress) jumps out of bed and departs. But even at this moment of complete collapse of love, deception has to be maintained in this through the looking glass world. The angry *puella* may have darted out of bed but 'lest her maids should know she was untouched, water covered the disgrace'. The girl is more shamed by sexual failure than adultery.

The smug winner of 2.2 is the tortured cheated lover of 3.14, prey to a *puella* who has employed the tactics that Ovid had educated her in throughout Books One and Two. She has in a calculated method become accomplice to her own surrender, but what Ovid implies with his increasingly bleak and humourless amatory work is that love as conquest has become love as domination, an ugly game of power in which there are no winners. In such an environment, love fails.

Love and politics cannot be, and are not, kept separate. This might be the most discomfiting message of all in this increasingly bleak collection. We have already discussed occasions such as 1.2 and 2.12 where Cupid and Ovid, respectively, take on distinctly imperial postures in their triumphs of love. After all, *Amores* 1.1 starts with an act of imperialism: Eros annexing the poet's skill into his territory. It can be, and has been, suggested that with the *Amores*, Ovid delivers a very unsettling political message that is not just advocating a licentious style of life. Hostility and competition in love increases as we progress through the *Amores*; so does uneasiness at the consequences of domination. Controlled tightly by her oppressive pursuer, the girl replies in kind, to prove the success (and condemned nature) of Ovid's elegiac project. But the putatively alternative world of elegy has become corrupt. There is no elegiac pause and no escape. Ovid's afternoon daydream of Corinna in 1.5, a quietness and a loving consummation of sorts, has been transformed in a world in which everyone is an adulterer and in which all compete in love.

The imperialism of the corrupt world has permeated the world of love and rendered the lover impotent. There is no truth in a world in which the lover knows that his girl is untrue, but commits himself to pretend that she is true in spite of all that he can see. Love *has* become war, and not its alternative. War dehumanises all involved: winners turn into victims and the other way round. But in this transformation of love there is commentary on the real world into which Ovid is drawn: a world of competition, dishonesty and lack of commitment to one's fellow. This is a world which drives lovers apart and in which Corinna is but a memory amidst pervasive corruption and violence. There is a reason why Cupid has taken to the triumphal chariot of Augustus in *Amores* 1.2: the corruption of the political has absorbed the promise of love.

5

Nomadic Love in Ovid's *Amores*

The focus of this book has been the personal poems of love produced by the Roman elegists. I have been interested in showing how being in – and talking about being in – love becomes for the Latin love poets a way of talking about one's self, one's position in society, one's art and ultimately one's politics. It has been suggested by others that Latin love elegy was inevitably a short-lived genre: fuelled by anger and the need for protest and subversive debate as the Republic turned to Empire, it no longer had scope to flourish, once Augustus' sovereignty expanded and tightened its grip on society. Ovid's presumed exile and his death away from Rome brings the curtain down on this intense personal poetry of love and Rome; a genre that has been sent into exile.

Unlike his predecessors, Ovid had, in fact, known no other leader than Augustus, no other regime than Empire. Writing decades after the consolidation of power in the hand of the emperor, the new regime had become a fact of life to which there could be no effective opposition, anymore than we can oppose the weather. Yet, the regime was still open to satirical attack.

I finish this introduction to Latin love by looking backwards, offering a reading from the exile to the lover. What I would hope to leave lingering after the end of elegy is the observation that even before exile, Ovid was a nomad of love and Rome was no longer a home for the lover. Indeed, to a lesser or greater degree, all Latin love elegy is a nomadic mode of expression and existence. Our authors are never fixed and they are always changing. They never resolve the problems and no elegiac corpus ends with our prince marrying his princess and living happily ever after in his castle. Instead, the elegiac lovers find themselves in the margins of society, and any settling is resisted.

Mobility provides the poets with an external vantage point from which they can see Roman society, but somehow remain apart from it.

It is this nomadic elegy that finds echoes in two celebrated modern reimaginings of Ovid in exile: David Malouf's *An Imaginary Life* and Christoph Ranmayr's rather dense and unsettling *Last World*, both of which treated Ovid as the iconic poet of exile rather than his more celebrated and glittering persona of the lover. Ovid in both novels is asked to speak for the modern condition from the position of the outcast struggling to control his language and communication.

In Malouf's *Imaginary Life*, published in the late 1970s, Ovid meets a wild boy outside Tomis on the Black Sea. The poet and the boy immerse themselves in storytelling, struggling through their linguistic differences and mismatched knowledge of their world(s) to establish an authority, coherence and communicable meaning for their own biographies. When Ovid brings the boy into the town of Tomis, he disturbs the hierarchies of the place, since the boy clearly does not belong there; the boy soon finds that he has to uproot and Ovid follows his wild companion out beyond the city into the 'natural' habitat. This might seem a second exile: the first from the cosmopolitan centre, the second from its provincial counterpart, into the total wilderness (and lack of civilization) around Tomis. Ovid had attempted to establish a modicum of order in Tomis to mitigate partially his exile. Yet, he is faced with problems of communication, and his desire to make contact with, and meaning of, the wild and weird boy drives him into continuous displacement and retreat from Rome and all that it represents.

A similar fascination with the exilic condition as inextricably tied with the quest for knowledge and self-invention runs through Christoph Ransmayr's prize-winning novel of the early 1990s. There are very few historical identifiers in this centrifugal novel. Everyone and everything is distorted somehow with an unfamiliarity which nonetheless sharpens the senses. Cotta, the protagonist, travels through a near-apocalyptic, wasted landscape in search of the banished poet Ovid and his burned manuscript of the *Metamorphoses* (which the

Roman poet had managed to destroy upon learning of his banishment). We soon realise that the world of the *Metamorphoses* and its celebrated figures have spilled out of Ovid's fictional work and into Cotta's world, a bizarre, uncanny version of Tomis, which only adds to the reader's, and Cotta's, own sense of alienation. We also realise that Cotta's quest for Ovid is also a quest for himself, a search for his identity, in a world of continuous flux.

Yet, Cotta's journey of self-knowledge is in itself an exile. Tomis' residents are all exiles in a landscape dominated by chaos. In Tomis, even the seasons do not behave with the expected regularity, time (as well as space) at both micro- and macro-levels being in confusion. The novel gradually yields up a few moments of recognition, but only a few, so we are never able to relax our intellectual effort for understanding this world. The author gives us just enough insight, just enough of a hint that order and comprehensibility will eventually emerge from the landscape to strengthen our resolve to carry on with the story; the promise of self-discovery, of a settlement of the tensions within the landscape (temporal and physical), encourages us on.

In both these stories, exile becomes the dominant mode of existence and a metaphor for the never-ending quest of knowledge, divested of reassuring familiarities and set points of reference. In both novels, exile ceases to be loss, as it would appear to be in the biographical tradition on Ovid, developing instead into a condition that is fundamental to the artistic drive. While ostentatiously speaking about Ovid's exile, Malouf's and Ransmayr's novels introduce us to a poet's exilic posture, a simulated exile marked by a degree of habitual detachment. Such a stance is a familiar one to us. It is often present in the work of the 'new nomads' that make up our contemporary diasporas, and who have become such an important ingredient of modern intelligentsias around the world. The 'condition', as it were, is eloquently discussed by Eva Hoffmann, a Polish-born émigré writer, living and working in the United States since her adolescence, in her contribution to a lecture series by immigrant intellectuals organised in New York in 1999:

What is at stake is not only, not even primarily actual exile but our preferred psychic positioning, so to speak, how we situate ourselves in the world. And these days we think the exilic position has precisely the virtues of instability, marginality, absence and outsiderness. (45)

A little later on in her lecture, acknowledging that most cases of self-exile are a fascinating combination of inevitability and intentionality, Hoffman nonetheless speaks out for the acquired advantages:

Being deframed, so to speak, from everything familiar, makes for a certain fertile detachment and gives one new ways of observing, seeing. This perhaps is the greatest advantage, for a writer of exile, the compensation for the loss and the formal bonus – that it gives you a perspective, a vantage point. (50)

For the rest of the chapter, I would like to explore this vantage point, the valorisation of absence and instability, the nomadic posture in Ovid's *Amores*. If the Ovidian persona has furnished the modern nomads with a poignant programme of exilic inspiration, if the literary exile thrives in acts of self-invention, would it not make sense for us to search for vestiges of this intellectual and emotional nomadism in the innovatory verse of Ovid's youth?

Our search needs patience. The reader's attention is more easily drawn to the polemic and self-congratulatory tone that dominates so much of the collection. Love, or more precisely, getting your girl, is an act of war which for Ovid results in his public (and literary) triumph in *Amores* 2.12. But rather than use the occasion to celebrate his centrality in the subverted traditions, Ovid asks: what is the use of being the general of a real battle? What use was it to Agamemnon that Troy fell, if he was to meet his death upon return to the Argolid? In contrast, Ovid's victory is safe, undisputed, personal and not based on luck. But if we read with a view to the larger picture, which I am about to do, we gradually realise that Ovid's world is a fleeting one and the security of his victory is evanescent. There is to be no triumph, no ending, no resolution, no coming home.

In *Amores* 2.16 we would be excused in thinking we witness a moment of return, a *nostos*:

> I am held at Sulmo, a third of the Pelignan countryside;
> small, but a region with healthy, irrigating water.
> Even though the summer sun, from close up, cleaves the earth
> and the impudent star of Orion's dog flashes,
> fresh waters roam through the fields of Sulmo
> and fertile glass grows in soft ground.
>
> 2.16.1–6

A retreat to the countryside, the sound of the running water, lusciousness, shade, the midday heat in a midsummer's day: is this the pastoral, poetic arcadia, and a moment before the *puella*'s epiphany? Ovid is swift in denying the homecoming:

> But my flame is away – I got one word wrong! –
> What kindles the fire is far away; the fire is here.
>
> 2.16.11–12

Ovid has not arrived home, his girl is not there, and no place is home without his travelling *puella*. The *nostos* is not complete, even though, as soon as his girl (the 'Penelope' of his particular *Odyssey*) turns up, surely the charm of the small house in Sulmo will be irresistible.

Or will it? The conclusion of the narrative remains open, but we already know that Ovid is suspicious of the lures of a home or a place that might seduce this travelling man: 'even if I were given a place between Castor and Pollux, without you I would not want to be anywhere in heaven' (2.16.13–14). The devotion to the *puella* should, of course, not be underestimated, but the rejection of a home among the gods (a final resolution and resting place as a god, alongside Jupiter and Hercules and, perhaps more controversially, Julius Caesar, and possibly next to the seat being kept for Augustus) speaks volumes for the contrast between love and fixity. Indeed, after a rather perfunctory complaint about the existence of roads that encourage lovers to separate, Ovid reverses to revel in the road's potential and reveals a utopia which involves no pastoral or Tibullan rural retreat:

> Then, if I, frightful and unkempt, pressed on through the windy Alps,
> as long as I was with my girl, the journey would still be easy;
> With my girl I would dare to break through Syrtes' quicksands
> and open full sails to take on the unkind south wind.

> And I would fear neither the omens that Scylla barks out of her
>   virginal groin
> nor your bays, curved Cape Malea,
> nor the rushing water that Charybdis' mouth, sated with ship-wrecks,
> spews and, having poured it out, then sucks back in again.

> Because, if the windy might of Neptune triumphs
> and the waves carry away the gods that help us,
> throw your snow-white arms around my shoulders
> and I will bear the lovely burden with my agile body.

2.16.19–30

In this description of the lovers' union, the images of happiness are built on movement. Howling winds and gigantic waves are rendered in a world of violence, divinity and uncertainty which would seem to contrast with the certainty of the lovers, but which also seem necessary for the lovers to be united. The lovers meet and separate at the whim of the natural elements, and Ovid should not really be as content to ride the waves with his beloved. As he himself finds out elsewhere in the *Amores,* natural elements are unreliable; they will not always conspire to bring the two lovers together. Poem 3.6 is a case in point. A swollen river has burst its banks and Ovid is cut off from his beloved because there is no bridge or rope ferry to get him across. Ovid appears furious and calls the river names. The river is a nobody, without home and ancestry, a low-birth in the world of the rivers:

> What is your problem with me, wild river? Why do you
> delay shared joys? Why, rude one, break the journey that I have started?
> Why? If you were running like a proper river, or you were a famous one,

and if your reputation was the greatest throughout the world –
but you have no name: a gathering of falling streams,
and you have neither source nor home, nor a steady route of yours.
For source you have the rain and melted snow,
the riches that dull winter provides you with.

3.6.87–94

But if nobility of birth and the lack of home are being used as an affront against the recalcitrant river, the very same credentials are repeatedly and emphatically rejected in 2.16, which we looked at above. When read against Ovid's indifference to his home, his ancestry, his birthplace (an indifference twice stated in no uncertain terms in 2.16), the river's lack of appreciation of what home and belonging actually mean encourages the reader to place the two vagabonds alongside each other. Though he is protesting against the river's instability, water tides and river flows seem to be much closer to Ovid's heart than his affected attack on the unhelpful river of 3.6 would have us believe. A ship lurching from bank to bank is, in fact, the image he chooses in order to convey his inability to pick one of the two available girls in 2.10. Only that there the dilemma is, of course, fake and the poet is happy to continue like a ship rocking from side to side, enjoying one *puella* and then the next: 'if one girl can be enough for me: if not, then I will take both' (2.10.22).

The wide, blue ocean may take its toll on the lovers, but it offers its compensations too. Poem 2.11 plays wittily with, and twists, our expectations. The *puella* is going away leaving a sad poet-lover stranded at the shore. Yet, a sad beginning is compensated by a happy ending and a fulfilling closure, and that surely makes for a promising love story. Filled with ecstasy at the safe return of his girl, the poet welcomes her back, only too keen to accept her account of her trip, not in the least interested in checking its veracity.

There sitting next to me, you will tell me many tales, sipping wine –
How your ship was nearly wrecked in the midst of the ocean
and, while you were rushing back to me, how neither the hostile

nights nor the wild southern winds scared you.
I will take them all as true, even though they will be fiction.
Why should not I please myself with my own wishes?

2.11.49–54

Is this the moment of Ovid's *nostos*, the poet's homecoming, that keeps eluding us, the moment when Ovid stops fleeing, having found his own coastline home, a centre in the margins to juxtapose to the public narrative and the demands of Rome? Indeed, the happy end is guaranteed in more than one way in this concluding scene of 2.11: the lover's physical union is bolstered with a narrative (the girl's) that cements the connection with an audience (the poet's) wholly determined to receive the story as an emotional and poetic arrival, on top of the literal one. The story may be a lie, but who cares?

And yet, the hypothesis appears less secure once we start exploring the middle part of the poem. As the girl disappears over the horizon, countless voices fill the narrative with tales of howling winds, swollen seas and stormy rocks below wild mountains.

Let others tell you stories of battling winds,
which waters Scylla and which Charybris molest,
from what rocks the violent Ceraunian mountains stand out
the bay where Syrtes' small and large quicksands lie hidden.
Let others report these to you; and what each one says, believe!
No gale can harm him who has faith.

2.11.17–22

As these stories steal the focus away from the girl's journey, the apparent solidity of the love story is put to question. Time and space dissolve, the *puella* retreats and what dominates the stage is a series of tales celebrating constant change and journeys into the unknown. As the girl's departure blends with these other similar, and compelling, epic tales of the big wide blue, we are beginning to come to terms with the poet's reality: a lover's journey is an enchanting adventure on paper, a figment of poetic imagination.

Despite its happy ending, *Amores* 2.11 is in fact a rather exquisite case study of the poet nomad who never arrives, never rests. We are met in the beginning of the poem with the poet-lover's declarations of devoted love and we are signed off with the rare image of a reunited couple celebrating the endurance of this love at the seaside: no sign of the usual obstacles that tend to keep the lovers apart in Ovid's world; no escorts, no husband, no door to block the way. But as we delve into the poem the certainty vanishes. Ostensibly solid and safe emotions appear to be written on the sand, literally and metaphorically, as the two lovers' reunion dissipates inside a web of poetic reflections and poetic creations that actually keep the couple apart. Corinna's journey is one of many such tales of howling winds and raging storms out there, some of them imagined by the girl herself, an exercise on paper and a good excuse to give the two lovers a break. Their separation provides the space and the time for other stories to interrupt, compete with, belie, but also complement Ovid's and his girl's story of love and affection, making sure no homecomings are ever convincing in Ovid's nomadic imagination.

* * *

Amores 2.11 is by no means the sole example of a life and a love story without a home, without a centre in the *Amores*. As we progress along the books, the topographical realities of Ovid's world and love affair with Corinna become increasingly fleeting, a world gradually crossing itself out of the map. The third book of the *Amores* seems particularly indifferent to either attacking Rome's hostile centre or cultivating a counter-life in the margins.

Poem 3.2 takes place in a circus, and more particularly in the spectators' stands. We are right in the middle of this most public of spaces and times. Surrounded by crowds, the lover, one would think, could avail himself of one of two options: either make a gesture of public defiance by somehow demonstrating his special bond with the girl, or succumb to public expectations and sit quietly apart from her.

Our lover, unsurprisingly, goes a third way: though inscribed in the middle of public life, Ovid's poem essentially refuses to engage with it. The action is fervently paced as Ovid issues instructions left, right and centre:

> You, though, on the right here, whoever you are, be careful
> with my girl: you hurt her as your side presses onto her.
> And you who watches over our heads, draw your legs back,
> and do not press her back with your hard knees, if you have any shame.
>
> 3.2.21–4

The stream of consciousness continues unabated all the way to the 84th, and last, line of the poem. Ever solicitous of his girl, the poet attends to the closest details in need of attending, lifts her dress, dusts her lap, and then issues frantic advice to the charioteer of the *puella's* favourite horse as to how he can secure his win, and the *puella's* satisfaction. The horse indeed wins, but Ovid has little to celebrate: 'My girl's hopes are redeemed; my hopes are still waiting to be fulfilled' (3.2.81). If this sudden suggestion of sadness surprises anyone, they should read the whole poem again more carefully. In the course of this day out at the circus, the only real interaction between Ovid and his *puella* is fleeting, if promising: 'She laughed; and with these sparkling eyes she promised something. That is enough here. You can pay back the rest somewhere else' (3.2.83–4).

Amores 3.4 adds to this timeless and spaceless love story, as Ovid turns the tables on stable marriage, fidelity, chastity and a whole lot of similar celebrated attitudes of the establishment. But, again, this is not the defiant celebration of Ovid in opposition to a centre of power that we might expect. Instead of 'the naughty life is the good life', we get 'the good life is actually the naughty life'. In the beginning the poet sets out to confuse and win over the girl's escort and guard. The girl who gets closely guarded may seem chaste, but actually is not:

> You brutal man, guarding a soft girl leads you nowhere;
> her own good disposition must be her guard.

If a girl is chaste, without fear, this girl is truly chaste;
but she who does not do because she mustn't, she will somehow do it.

3.4.1–4

And the case for this is gradually built in the course of the poem: 'he who is allowed to sin, sins less; the licence debilitates the seeds of immorality' (3.4.9–10). In any case, this confinement is not in accordance with Roman propriety: a free Roman girl, forfeiting her freedom in the name of chastity resembles too much a foreign import. And accepting the rein from her guard (which given the combination of power and sex is surely in itself a sexual image) equally surely upsets social order: the *puella* is beholden to and takes orders from a slave (3.4.33–6) and in this there is a reversal in which rules of power and sex are perverted. Lastly, the husband is invited to see the incongruity and adjust his role:

And cultivate the friends – the many friends – your wife will bring you;
a great favour will come to you with almost no effort:
you will always be able to enter the parties of the young
and see her with many gifts that you did not give her at home.

3.4.45–8

In this topsy-turvy world, it is more Roman to abolish the girl's guard. The *Lex Julia*, in fact, adds spice and thus encourages adultery. The guard should go and the husband had better act as a pimp, welcoming the girl's friends, if there is ever any chance of the flame of illicit love to die out. The advice to allow the girl to sleep with the poet in order to encourage her chastity seems delivered deadpan, perverting the relationship between husband and poetic lover. *Amicitia* (friendship), which was central to how one got on in Roman society, was to be achieved through the wife's bed. The honour of the husband would be achieved through the wife's adultery. But, of course, such behaviour is represented as a norm of Roman society and the man who expects his wife to be chaste becomes perverse. Systematically divesting expressions/representatives of Roman order of their certainties, Ovid manages to bring adultery right into the centre of the Augustan regime, turning adultery into a major mechanism for establishing Roman social relations. Adultery becomes pervasive; it is in the mind, maybe inside the house, maybe outside it, maybe in the Forum, maybe in the circus, and, at the same time, nowhere in particular, thus making it very difficult for the emperor to root it out.

The poem straight after this, 3.5, is the description of a dream the poet had one night in his sleep. Seeking shelter from the heat he was sitting under an oak tree, when a fine white cow came and stood before his eyes, whiter than first snow and the milk only just oozing from the cow's udders. Admiring the cow, the poet noticed that she was lying next to a bull, a happy image of two lovers on the grass interrupted by a crow that came and settled next to them, probing the cow's white chest with his beak three times. Puzzled by the apparition, the poet needs a dream interpreter to have his dream explained. Apparently, the cow is his girl and he is the bull. But the cow will go and the bruise on her chest indicates adultery. Dreams, metaphors, disguises of many forms, are now used to map out the Ovidian love story, in a world that feels, and is, a very long way away from the materiality of Rome.

*   *   *

Let me round up. Towards the end of *An Imaginary Life*, Ovid and the Child, the strange creature he met in the fields around Tomis, are preparing to cross the river and enter the real wilderness. As Ovid himself puts it: 'I am going out now into the unknown, the real unknown, compared with which Tomis was but a degenerate outpost of Rome, and am, I believe, following the clear path of my fate' (135). Ovid can hardly contain his excitement:

> always to be pushing out like this, beyond what I know cannot be the limits – what else should a man's life be? … What else should our lives be but a continual series of beginnings, of painful settings out into the unknown, pushing off from the edges of consciousness into the mystery of what we have not yet become except in dreams that blow in

from out there bearing the fragrance of islands we have not yet sighted in our walking hours. (135)

Willing and weak at the same time, the poet lets the Child push him on to a land and a future that are increasingly hazy, increasingly hard to delineate. The poet marvels at the Child's energy and determination:

He is full of it, of some suppressed passion for the furthest reaches of what he can see, and I feel that, glowing in him, as he stoops to bring me whatever he has found for us to eat. (149)

The relationship between the poet and the Child has now taken the form of a soft and tender kinship. The boy guides the poet to a land and a life beyond expression, all the way caring and concerned about the frail man. The poet marvels at the blend of so close affinity and so much incomprehension: 'And yet for all his closeness, he seems more and more to belong to a world that lies utterly beyond me, and beyond my human imagining' (149).

Haunted by this land he can hardly see in the distance, Ovid retreats to the realm of sleep and dreaming. As in *Amores* 3.5, he gently slides into an unfamiliar land that confuses him as it reveals its secrets to him.

I lie down to sleep and wonder if, in the looseness of sleep, I might not strike down roots along all the length of my body, and as I enter the first dream, almost feel it begin to happen. (147)

In this journey to the unknown, the dreams speak to him in a language that he cannot use when awake. Ovid thinks of and tells us often of his dreams. The Child agitates him and enthuses him in equal measure. And he wonders how he can be so close and yet so separate from the Child:

Who is he, this Child who leads me deeper into the earth, further from the far, safe place where I began …? Where has he come from? Out of which life? Out of which time? Did I really discover him out there in the pinewoods, or did he somehow discover me, or rediscover me, out of my own alienation from the world of men? Is he the Child of my first days under the olive trees at Sulmo? Is it the same Child? Is there, after all, only one? And where is he leading me, since I know at last that it is he who is the leader, he now who is inducting me into the mysteries of a world I have never for a moment understood. (145)

Embodied in the weird and wonderful Child is a desire for adventure in a faraway land, always there inside the poet since his first days under the olive trees at Sulmo, his father's green land. And that faraway land does not obey the normal rules of space and time.

> I no longer ask myself where we are making for. The notion of a desti-
> nation no longer seems necessary to me. It has been swallowed up in
> the immensity of this landscape, as the days have been swallowed up
> by the sense I now have of a life that stretches beyond the limits of
> measurable time. (144)

Reading the *Amores* again, having read Malouf's *An Imaginary Life*, we can now see with more clarity what it was that sent Ovid on a continuous journey through the *Amores*. It was not the exile to modern day Costanza that was the grandest adventure of Ovid's life. It is explicitly not Tomis at the Black Sea shore that is being talked about in the extracts from Malouf's novel that we explored earlier in this chapter. That place, a dull, restrictive, degenerative outlet of Rome, Ovid leaves behind as he crosses the river preparing to enter the steppes with the boy. It is, instead, an external pull and an internal drive, and an urge latent inside him since his childhood days that sets him on the course of a nomad's existence. It is the escape into the wilderness and beyond the confines of the map that questions the centrality of Augustus' imperial rule. Even as adultery takes over all the spaces of Rome and becomes the social norm, so the poet is driven from the centre into another world, a world of dreams, of non-place, indifferent to geography. The to-be-exiled Ovid was already in the *Amores* preparing his exile, long before word came from the offended emperor.

If life in the margins has been established as a signature Ovidian gesture, what we find in the *Amores* is a life *and* a love without home. There is a detachment that underwrites every line in this poetry of love. Ovid does not belong to Augustus' Rome: we knew as much, but what we realise is that he does not belong to adulterous Rome either. The irony-coated, highly stylised presentation of victory in love only thinly disguises an eye hungry for a distant vantage point, that formalised advantage for the outsider that Eva Hoffmann raised awareness of when speaking of her semi-voluntary exile in the United States, as we saw early on in this chapter. Ovid cultivates his visions of Rome but from a distant vantage point of alienation in which the absurdities of Rome become a dance in which the poet neither wishes nor is able to participate.

Further Reading

The list below includes a mix of first contact points and more advanced writings on the authors (and particularly on the specific books) that I discussed in my study. It is far from exhaustive but I believe it offers the newcomer the tools for a more sustained engagement with this poetry.

On Augustan politics and culture

Galinsky, Karl. *Augustan Culture. An Interpretive Introduction* (Princeton: Princeton University Press, 1996).

Habinek, Thomas. *The Politics of Latin Literature: Writing, Identity, and Empire in Ancient Rome* (Princeton: Princeton University Press, 1998).

Hallett, Judith. 'Women as Same and Other in Classical Roman Elite', *Helios* 16 (1989): 59–78.

Ross, David. *Backgrounds to Augustan Poetry* (Cambridge: Cambridge University Press, 1975).

Wallace-Hadrill, Andrew. '*Mutatio morum*: The Idea of a Cultural Revolution', in Thomas Habinek and Alessandro Schiesaro (eds), *The Roman Cultural Revolution* (Cambridge: Cambridge University Press, 1997), 3–22.

—*Rome's Cultural Revolution* (Cambridge: Cambridge University Press, 2008).

Zanker, Paul. *Power of Images in the Age of Augustus*, translated by Alan Shapiro (Ann Arbor: Michigan University Press, 1990).

On Latin love elegy in general

Fredrick, David. 'Reading Broken Skin: Violence in Roman Elegy', in Judith Hallett and Marilyn Skinner (eds), *Roman Sexualities* (Princeton: Princeton University Press, 1997), 172–93.

Gardner, Hunter. *Gendering Time in Augustan Love Elegy* (Oxford: Oxford University Press, 2013).

Gold, Barbara. *A Companion to Roman Love Elegy* (Malden, MA and Oxford: Blackwell Publishing, 2012).

Greene, Ellen. *The Erotics of Domination: Male Desire and the Mistress in Latin Love Elegy* (Baltimore: Johns Hopkins University Press, 1998).

James, Sharon. 'Her Turn to Cry: The Politics of Weeping in Roman Love Elegy', *Transactions of the American Philological Association* 133 (2003): 99–122.

Kennedy, Duncan. *The Arts of Love. Five Studies in the Discourse of Roman Love Elegy* (Cambridge: Cambridge University Press, 2003).

Lyne, R. O. A. M. *The Latin Love Poets from Catullus to Horace* (Oxford: Clarendon Press, 1980).

Miller, Allen Paul. *Subjecting Verses. Latin Love Elegy and the Emergence of the Real* (Princeton and Oxford: Princeton University Press, 2004).

—(ed.). *Latin Erotic Elegy. An Anthology and a Reader* (London: Routledge, 2002).

Miller, Allen Paul and Platter, Chuck (eds). *Power, Politics and Discourse in Augustan Elegy*, Special Issue of *Classical World* 92.5 (1999).

Rea, Jennifer A. *Legendary Rome: Myths, Monuments, and Memory on the Palatine and Capitoline* (London: Duckworth, 2007 (chapters on Tibullus and Propertius)).

Veyne, Paul. *Roman Erotic Elegy: Love, Poetry, and the West,* translated by David Pellauer (Chicago: University of Chicago Press, 1988).

Wyke, Maria. 'Mistress and Metaphor in Augustan Elegy', *Helios* 16 (1989): 25–47.

—'Taking the Woman's Part: Engendering Roman Love Elegy', in A. J. Boyle (ed.), *Roman Literature and Ideology:* Ramus *Essays for J. P. Sullivan* (Bendigo, Australia: Aureal Punlications, 1995), 110–28; revised and reprinted as 'Taking the Woman's Part: Gender and Scholarship on Love Elegy', in Maria Wyke, *The Roman Mistress* (Oxford: Oxford University Press, 2002), 155–91.

On Catullus

Ancona, Ronnie. *Writing Passion. A Catullus Reader* (Mundelein, IL: Bolchazy-Carduzzi Publishers, 2004).

Finamore, J. F. 'Catullus 50 and 51: Friendship, Love, and Otium', *Classical World* 78 (1984): 11–19.

Fitzgerald, William. *Catullan Provocations. Lyric Poerty and the Drama of Position* (Berkeley: University of California Press, 1995).

Gaisser, Julia (ed.). *Catullus. Oxford Readings in Classical Studies* (Oxford: Oxford University Press, 2007).

Green, Ellen. 'Journey to the Remotest Meadow. A Reading of Catullus 11', *Intertexts* 1 (1997): 147–55.

Janan, Micaela. '*When the Lamp is Shattered*'. *Desire and Narrative in Catullus* (Carbondale, IL: Southern Illinois University Press, 1994).

Skinner, Marilyn. '*Ego Mulier*: The Construction of Male Sexual Identity in Catullus', *Helios* 20 (1993): 107–30; reprinted in J. Gaisser (ed.), *Catullus. Oxford Readings in Classical Studies* (Oxford: Oxford University Press, 2007), 447–75.

—*A Companion to Catullus* (Malden, MA and Oxford: Blackwell Publishing, 2007).

Wiseman, Peter. *Catullus and his World. A Reappraisal* (Cambridge: Cambridge University Press, 1985).

Wray, David. *Catullus and the Poetics of Roman Manhood* (Cambridge: Cambridge University Press, 2001).

On Tibullus

Boyd, Barbara. 'Parva Seges Satis Est: The Landscape of Tibullan Elegy in 1.1 and 1.10', *Transactions of the American Philological Association* 114 (1984): 273–80.

Drinkwater, Megan. '"His turn to cry". Tibullus' Marathus Cycle (1.4, 1.8, and 1.9) and Roman Elegy', *Classical Journal* 107 (2012): 423–50.

Leach, Eleanor Winsor. 'Poetics and Poetic Design in Tibullus' First Elegiac Book', *Arethusa* 13 (1980): 79–96.

Lee, Guy. '*Otium cum indignitate*: Tibullus 1.1,' in Tony Woodman and David West (eds), *Quality and Pleasure in Latin Poetry* (Cambridge: Cambridge University Press, 1974), 94–111.

Lee-Stecum, Parshia. *Powerplay in Tibullus: Reading Elegies Book One* (Cambridge: Cambridge University Press, 1988).

Lee-Stecum, Peter. 'Poet/Reader, Authority Deferred: Re-Reading Tibullan Elegy', *Arethusa* 33.2 (2000): 177–215.

Moore, Timothy. 'Tibullus 1.7: Reconciliation through Conflict', *Classical World* 82 (1989): 423–31.

Nikoloutsos, Konstantinos. 'The Boy as Metaphor: The Hermeneutics of
    Homoerotic Desire in Tibullus 1.9', *Helios* 38.1 (2011): 27–57.
—'From Tomb to Womb: Tibullus 1.1 and the Discourse of Masculinity in
    Post Civil War Rome', *Scholia* 20 (2011): 52–71.
Todd, Lee. 'The Potentials of Narrative: The Rhetoric of the Subjective in
    Tubullus', in Genevieve Liveley and Patricia Salzman (eds), *Latin Elegy
    and Narratology: Fragments of Story* (Columbus: Ohio State University
    Press, 2008), 196–222.
Wray, David. 'What Poets Do: Tibullus on 'Easy Hands', *Classical Philology* 98
    (2003): 217–50.

On Sulpicia

Flaschenriem, Barbara. 'Sulpicia and the Rhetoric of Disclosure', *Classical
    Philology* 94 (1999): 36–54.
Hallett, Judith. 'The Eleven Elegies of the Augustan Poet Sulpicia', in
    L. Churchill (ed.), *Women Writing Latin. From Roman Antiquity to Early
    Roman Europe*, Volume 1 (New York and London: Routledge, 2002),
    45–65.
Keith, Alison. 'Critical Trends in Interpreting Sulpicia', *Classical World* 100.1
    (2006): 3–10.
Skoie, Mathilde. 'Telling Sulpicia's Joys: Narrativity at the Receiving End', in
    Genevieve Liveley and Patricia Salzman (eds), *Latin Elegy and Narratology:
    Fragments of Story* (Columbus: Ohio State University Press, 2008), 241–56.

On Propertius (focusing mainly on books 1–3)

Booth, Joan. 'Problems and Programmatics in Propertius 1.1', *Hermes* 129
    (2001): 63–74.
Breed, W. Brian. 'Propertius on Not Writing about Civil Wars', in Brian Breed,
    Cynthia Damon and Andreola Rossi (eds), *Citizens of Discord. Rome and
    its Civil Wars* (Oxford: Oxford University Press, 2010), 233–48.
Dufallo, Basil. 'Propertian Elegy as Restored Behaviour. Evoking Cynthia and
    Cornelia', *Helios* 30.2 (2003): 163–79.

Fraschenriem, Barbara. 'Loss, Desire, and Writing in Propertius 1.19 and 2.15', *Classical Antiquity* 16 (1997): 259–77.

Greene, Ellen and Welch, Tara (eds). *Oxford Readings in Propertius* (Oxford: Oxford University Press, 2012).

Gold, Barbara K. 'Propertius 3.9: Maecenas as *Eques, Dux, Fautor*', in Barbara K. Gold (ed.), *Literary and Artistic Patronage in Ancient Rome* (Austin: University of Texas Press, 1982), 103–17.

—'How Women (Re)Act in Roman Love Poetry: Inhuman She-Wolves and Unhelpful Mothers in Propertius's Elegies', *Helios* 33.2 (2006): 165–87.

Johnson, W. R. *A Latin Lover in Ancient Rome. Readings in Propertius and His Genre* (Ohio: Ohio State University Press, 2009).

Keith, Alison. *Propertius. Poet of Love and Leisure* (London: Duckworth, 2008).

Nicholson, N. 'Bodies without Names, Names with Bodies: Propertius 1.21–22', *Classical Journal* 94 (1999): 143–61.

O'Neill, Kerill. 'The Lover's Gaze and Cynthia's Glance', in Ronnie Ancona and Ellen Greene (eds), *Gendered Dynamics in Latin Love Poetry* (Baltimore: Johns Hopkins University Press, 2005), 243–70.

Sharrock, Alison. 'Constructing characters in Propertius', *Arethusa* 33 (2000): 263–84.

Spelman, C. C. 'Propertius 2.3: The Chaos of Desire', *Arethusa* 32.1 (1999): 123–45.

Tatum, W. Jeffrey. 'Aspirations and Divagations: The Poetics of Place in Propertius 2.10', *Transactions of the American Philological Association* 130 (2000), 393–410.

Valladares, Hérica. 'The Lover as Model Viewer: Gendered Dynamics in Propertius 1.3', in Ronnie Ancona and Ellen Greene (eds), *Gendered Dynamics in Latin Love Poetry* (Baltimore: Johns Hopkins University Press, 2005), 243–70.

On Ovid's *Amores*

Armstrong, Rebecca. *Ovid and his Love Poetry* (London: Duckworth, 2005).

Boyd, Barbara. *Ovid's Literary Loves: Influence and Innovation in the Amores* (Ann Arbor: University of Michigan Press, 1997).

Buchan, Mark. '*Ovidius Imperamator*: Beginnings and Endings of Love
     Poems and Empire in the *Amores*', *Arethusa* 28 (1995): 53–85.
Cahoon, Leslie. 'The Bed as Battlefield. Erotic Conquest and Military
     Metaphor in Ovid's Amores', *Transactions of the American Philological
     Association* 118 (1988): 293–307.
Davis, P. J. 'Ovid's *Amores*: A Political Reading', *Classical Philology* 94 (1999):
     431–49.
Katz, Phyllis. 'Teaching the Elegiac Lover in Ovid's *Amores*', *The Classical
     World* 102 (2009): 163–67.
Liveley, Genevieve. *Ovid: Love Songs* (Bristol: Bristol Classical Press, 2005).
O'Gorman, Ellen. 'Love and the Family; Augustus and Ovidian Elegy',
     Arethusa 30.1 (1997): 103–24.
Salzman-Mitchell, Patricia. 'Snapshots of a Love Affair: *Amores* 1.5 and the
     Program of Elegiac Narrative', in Genevieve Liveley and Patricia Salzman
     (eds), *Latin Elegy and Narratology: Fragments of Story* (Columbus: Ohio
     State University Press, 2008), 34–50.
Sharrock, Alison. 'The Drooping Rose: Elegiac Failure in Amores 3.7', *Ramus*
     24 (1995): 152–80.
—'Ovid and the Discourses of Love: the Amatory Works', in Philip Hardie
     (ed.), *The Cambridge Companion to Ovid* (Cambridge: Cambridge
     University Press, 2002), 150–62.
Tracey, Valerie. 'Ovid's Self-portrait in the *Amores*', *Helios* 6 (1978): 57–62.
Wyke, Maria. 'Reading Female Flesh: *Amores* 3.1', in Peter Knox (ed.), *Oxford
     Readings in Ovid* (Oxford: Oxford University Press, 2006), 169–204.

Index